NEW DIMENSIONS IN HERBAL HEALING

The Wheelwright Legacy

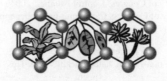

By
Jack Tips, N.D., Ph.D., C.C.N., C.Hom.

New Dimensions in Herbal Healing
The Wheelwright Legacy
© 2003 by Jack Tips/Apple-A-Day Service Group

For information address:
Apple-A-Day Press
1500 Village West Drive, Suite 77
Austin, Texas 77833-1977

www.apple-a-daypress.com

ISBN 0-929167-23-6

Library of Congress Control Number: 2004091742
Library of Congress Cataloging-In-Publication Data

Tips, Jack C.
New Dimensions in Herbal Healing,
non-fiction, natural health / Jack Tips
p. cm.
ISBN 0-929167-23-6
1. Natural health - herbology
2. Healing - clinical herbology

First Edition

Typesetting/Lay Out: Keith Bahlmann, Bahl Graphics
Proofreading: Janine Tips
Cover Art: Michael Wilby

Use of trademarked terms:
Bio-Command Formula and *Bio-Function Formula*
by permission of
Systemic Formulas, Inc., Ogden, Utah

This information is provided in good will for informational and
educational purposes only. It is intended only to be a
communication with fellow practitioners who practice the
healing principles taught by A.S. Wheelwright and the
Wheelwright Healing System. These discussions do not
constitute labeling for any products, and no claims of cure or
treatment are implied beyond the hypothetical discussion of
natural health philosophies.

Table of Contents

Preface

This is a book for practitioners, healers, and practitioner/healers.

I've wanted to write a book about Doc Wheelwright's unique insights on herbal healing for a long time. Something's held me back 'til now.

You see, Wheelwright was able to take the ordinary, garden-variety, handed-down-for centuries, lost-its-place (to the overwhelming onslaught of drugs), weird and wacky field of herbology (as most people know it); and transform it back into the true medicine for the healing of the world's peoples. It took a lot of savvy and experience combined with the futuristic insights of science to bring forth a new dimension in herbal healing—one that is no longer an anachronistic *alternative* to the frightening side-effects and failures of modern medicine; but one that is relevant to our times and its new challenges.

Wheelwright believed that truth was self-evident for those who had eyes to see and ears to hear. Over the years since Wheelwright left us his legacy of herbal and healing insights, a growing number of dedicated natural health practitioner/healers have found the truth of his theories, theorems, insights, and principles. Now, with years of confirmation and success at the clinical level, it's time to share the fundamentals of Wheelwright's profound discoveries.

I became a Wheelwright protégé during the last seven years of his amazing and colorful life. I "got it", little by little, through a process that was both learning and unlearning. But "getting it" is a bit different than "being or doing it." I was able to provide both an historic as well as a practical matrix to Wheelwright's work, as seen in the publications to date, but it took a little time to put it into practice - hence the wait.

Telling the story of the culmination of Wheelwright's 'better mousetrap' would be easy—it's simply a show-and-tell session—like you'd get with any person or company with a product to sell. But Wheelwright really wasn't about show-and-tell. Wheelwright possessed an overview—an innate and intimate relationship with life—that guided him past the myriad pitfalls and sidetracks that plague the natural health movement. He was always two steps and thirty-years ahead of his time. He not only built better mousetraps, he was also a pied piper that carried a message forth—one that could rid our lives of the vermin (both literal and figurative) that affect our bodies and minds.

Telling this story so the deeper, universal insights are properly included has taken years of clinical practice, much trial and error, some devil's advocacy, and many blessed successes. Thankfully, now it's time.

This is a book about the hairsbreadth between mediocrity and radiance.

The distance between a practitioner and a healer can be immense in some cases, and in others only a hairsbreadth. The practitioner has knowledge, skills and a system. A practitioner can do great things. The healer has an understanding/awareness of life-principles and an empathy/perception of the cause of a person's state of limited adapt-ability combined with the ability to elicit a movement toward optimal health (change in vibratory rate) in another person. A healer can do great things as well.

In the healing arts, this world contains 99.9% practitioners. The 0.1% healers are both rare and misunderstood, and thus largely ineffective, globally.

But to be a practitioner that dwells in a healing perception is to be truly effective. "Ah, there's the rub," as Master Bill would say—to be or not to be a practitioner (with well-honed skills and expertise) plus to be the healer with the understanding, insights, and compassion to set the stage for the healing change. So here's the pinnacle of the healing profes-sions—the practitioner/healer. Many practitioners have found that Wheelwright's research and resulting bio-energetic herbal/nutritional formulas help bridge the gap between being a practitioner and a healer, and thus help support the practitioner/healer pursuit.

This is a book for all practitioners, healers, and practitioner/healers of every persuasion and modality.

The purpose of this material is certainly to help practitioners practice well. But hopefully the crown of healing genius that Wheelwright wore, often unnoticed like an old slouch hat, will be revealed and contribute to the return of the "true medicine" to its rightful prominence.

To present Wheelwright's formulas without presenting some of his essential insights would simply cater to practitioners' seemingly perpetual need for better mousetraps only to have them slung and sprung at the hoard of symptoms plaguing humanity instead of piping the melody that can actually free humanity from so many of its ills. (I'm not naïve in hoping for great changes to come from these discourses, but I know it's right to expect the best.)

The knowledge about Wheelwright's amazing formulas has been quietly growing for years despite the jaded skepticisms of practitioners who think they've already found "the best" and feel justified in closing their minds; and the indoctrinations by companies seeking to hold practitioners in their fold, driven by their bottom line more than their top-line commitment to true healing. This book is not to indoctrinate practitioners about formulas that "are the so-called best", but to present the principles and understandings that Wheelwright applied—principles that inevitably help all practioners practice better regardless of their healing modality and tools of choice.

Thus this book is really about the healing principles that allow us to understand the body's innate processes of regeneration, adaptability, and vitality as an expression of life itself. And this noble mission is completely compatible with Wheelwright's research.

This book is parochial, but then again, it's really not.

In citing Wheelwright's formulas, this book might appear, superficially, to be parochial to his "line" or his "company." And that's certainly true—so please understand this before we start. This material is independent insights on Wheelwright's work and is not intended as literature or marketing for Systemic Formulas, Inc.—the company that meticulously manufactures Wheelwright's formulas.

Beyond the focus on Wheelwright's formulas, there is one exceptional caveat: Wheelwright's principles are universal. They are not limited to anyone's formulas or any type of practice. They take us deeper into the meaning of TRUE HEALING and ultimately what it means to be a "practitioner/healer" which is a phrase that defines Wheelwright better than any other adjective or epithet ascribed to him including biochemist, genius, free-spirit, tool-and-die maker, rabble-rouser, quantum physicist, herbalist, rascal, savant, rebel; iconoclast, and character—all of which colored his essential nature.

Here, you'll see that ole Doc Wheelwright left us quite a legacy. Not just his superb herbal formulas which have helped tens-of-thousands of people regain their health; but the true legacy of a way of thinking on a more thorough and comprehensive level. Wheelwright had a knack of thinking deeper, broader, and more universally. He was the child with the perpetual "WHY?" and he had an uncanny antenna for bull-hockey that spews forth from people who know what to think instead of how to think. These traits gave him the enviable and unique ability to think outside the box while knowing exactly where the box was.

I hope you find the secrets of Wheelwright's legacy in this book. It's not in knowing what herbs go with what herbs. It's not in knowing which herbs are anionic and which are cationic. Nor is it in knowing what is the energy frequency of the gizzard, thyroid ganectagezoit, or liver.

It's in …. well, you'll see.

Jack Tips 12/31/03

New Dimensions in Herbal Healing

The Wheelwright Legacy

By Jack Tips, N.D., Ph.D., C.C.N., C.Hom.

Abstract. Alexander Stuart "Doc" Wheelwright, PhD, a 20th-Century herbal researcher, shaped a new dimension in natural healing with revolutionary breakthroughs in herbology including 1) herbal polarization principles, 2) tissue frequency (bio-energetic) compatibility, 3) solutions to many of herbal medicine's limitations, and 4) the pinnacle of his research—the six Systemic Bio-Command formulas. Proper application of the Wheelwright Healing System provides the clinician an unprecedented degree of precision and comprehensiveness in herbal/nutritional therapies that produces faster, more thorough, and more consistent remedial results.

Definitions

Bio-Energy - The flowing resonance of all life forms. The distinct, unique, and measurable energy generated by living matter. Sometimes called, "vitality," or "ch'i." In the human spectrum of bio-energy, the higher frequencies express greater adaptability and health.

Bio-Command® Formula - an herbal combination designed by master herbalist A. Stuart Wheelwright that increases the effectiveness and restorative action of a Bio-Function formula (specific tissue nutrition) through enhanced assimilation, increased tissue receptivity, and most importantly, by specifying the direction and impact of the combined herbal matrix toward one of six specific cellular functions (commands). This allows the herbal practitioner greater precision in clinical applications of herbal medicine.

Bio-Function® Formula - a nutritive and therapeutic herbal combination, designed by A. Stuart Wheelwright, that has been 'tuned' to a specific tissue's bio-energetic resonance matrix. It is designed to support that specific tissue (organ, gland, body system), both biochemically and bio-energetically, to optimize its inherent function and performance, thus helping the body restore and maintain its most optimal health.

Herbal Polarization Principles - Wheelwright catalogued herbs according to three ionization potentials - 1) *anionic* (-) which supports the cells' anabolic, building, tissue-relaxing, base (alkaline) activities; 2) *cationic* (+) which stimulates cellular activities toward their inherent catabolic, cleansing, active, acid-cycle processes; and 3) *poly-ionic* (ø) which provides a balanced or tonic effect to a tissue or body system. The inherent polarization potential of an herb plays a critically important and determining role in how that herb behaves when combined with other herbs, as well as how the body responds, and thus is of paramount importance for formula effectiveness.

Tissue Frequency - The bio-energetic signature or resonance pattern (matrix) that defines a tissue's innate physiology and function; the defining energy matrix of a tissue upon which its cellular identity and functional systems are organized. It is the resonance matrix, unique and measurable, of the tissue's innate, intelligent organizational structure based on the tissue's archetypal blueprint.

Wheelwright Healing System - a technique of comprehensive herbal, nutritional, and bio-energetic therapy that simultaneously provides multi-faceted support for 1) the body's constitutional state; 2) the tissue's biochemistry, bio-energy, specific functions, and cellular integrity; plus 3) tissue nourishment; 4) specific xenobiotic[1], toxic chemical/metal, and pathogenic involvements, 5) the underlying terrain (pH); 6) drainage of metabolic and other waste products; with application of the 7) Bio-Command directive. The Wheelwright Healing System is known for helping the body heal more rapidly and thoroughly.

---

[1] Xenobiotic — A completely synthetic chemical compound which does not naturally occur on earth and thus believed to be resistant to environmental degradation.

Introduction to a New Dimension in Herbal Medicine

Featuring Five Discourses on the Wheelwright Herbal Research and Healing System

In the past, health concerns mostly revolved around infections, wounds, acute diseases, plagues, and malnutrition. Today, we still have those ancient, fundamental concerns, oftentimes in different guise; but we now have the added confusions of 1) xenobiotic and other toxic agents (chemicals, heavy metals, preservatives, food additives, industrial pollutants, pesticides, household cleaners, anti-perspirants, second-hand smoke, petrochemicals, etc.); 2) errant application of vaccinations that confuse the immune system and introduce toxic levels of mercury into infants bodies; 3) radiations (nuclear, electro-magnetic, etc.) that mutate cells and proliferate cancerous activity; and 4) new, resistant strains of pathogens to further challenge the adaptability of the human vital force to maintain optimal health.

These new environmental challenges are coupled with the severe bankruptcy of today's food-nutrition with its proliferation of altered, empty-calorie, "quick-and-the-dead" foods that fail to provide our bodies with the fundamental nutrients they need to express optimal health.

Into this maelstrom of environmental pollution and nutritional impoverishment entered a champion who found a way to re-introduce the natural remedies, nutrition and lifestyle factors that our bodies crave for proper health. That champion was Alexander Stuart "Doc" Wheelwright, a biochemist and herbal researcher who applied the principles of quantum physics to the ancient science of herbology.

In the natural model of health, we find that the body is designed to heal itself provided there is no obstruction to cure. Obstructions can be congestions of blood and lymph, as well as bio-energy. But today, more than ever, our bodies are subjected to countless toxic and unnatural substances that stress its operating systems and inhibit its ability to maintain itself. When uncomfortable and painful symptoms appear and herald the body's distress, people seek help in correcting the pain or discomfort.

It is unfortunate that, all too often, people turn to suppressive, medical drugs to makes the symptom go away. It is unfortunate because suppressive drugs only push the disease in deeper (under the rug, so to speak) into the person's vitality. Since the symptom is suppressed and the cause not addressed, the disease will express itself in a more disturbing manifestation later. Thus we see the rise of chronic, degenerative diseases in those who, in ignorance of natural law, too frequently submit to the manipulation of their bodies with drugs. We also see the terrible, life-shortening side effects of drugs as well as the derangement of the body by interactions of different drugs.

On the other hand, in the natural health model, we have clear and well-proven methods to restore the body to optimal health—methods that assist the body in curing its ailments according to the principles of natural law rather than having drugs dictate a suppressive action.

In the natural health, alternative system of healing, we are preoccupied with treating the person, not the disease. We are preoccupied with the cause of the symptom much more than the symptom itself.

Wheelwright discovered how to take the age-old medicine of herbology and refine it into a powerful healing system that can address the complex, oftentimes daunting, modern-day challenges to our lives and quality of life. For this reason, he is credited with bringing herbology into the 21st-Century.

In this assembly of discourses, we will examine the Wheelwright Legacy, contemplate his far-reaching concepts, and learn how to apply them in clinical practice for the betterment of all people. Welcome to the Wheelwright Legacy.

Discourse 1:
The Bio-Command Formulas of
A.S. "Doc" Wheelwright

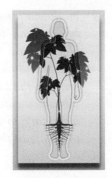

In starting with the Wheelwright Bio-Command formulas we are starting with the apex of his research, which might seem to be putting the cart before the horse, so to speak. But let's start with this compelling accomplishment so we have an idea of the magnitude of his work, and then backtrack through his research to understand how he arrived at this point and how it adds a powerful dimension to the Wheelwright Healing System.

Wheelwright's research and its resulting development of six Bio-Command formulas advanced herbal medicine into a new era of effectiveness largely because it solved not only the never-ending quest for natural therapies that work, but because it solved the major challenges that herbal medicine has faced over the centuries. Even more importantly, his research specifically addresses the challenges of "our time" in that today's health concerns are not the same as yesterday's.

The Systemic Bio-Command Formulas® are a unique dimension in herbology. Nowhere else in herbology, and certainly with no other patent formulas, is found anything resembling the Systemic Bio-Command formulas or the clinical results they bring. The closest herbal practice to the Bio-Command concept occurs in traditional Chinese herbology where a basic mixture of herbs (hub) can be altered for a more specific effect by the addition of other compatible herbs. This is the concept of '*herbal compounding*'. But only in Wheelwright's Bio-Command research do we find both the enhancement of the original hub formula and the alteration for a specific effect occurring simultaneously. This is because of his applications of quantum physics and the resulting ability to provide a bio-energetic boost that elicits the body's own healing trend.

"Health is, as life is, a balanced, perfect system. The secret of herbal healing is in the vibratory rate of the innate structures of plants. As life forms, plants organize according to the secret

mathematics of Life, and they can impart foundational healing information to the fundamental structures of a human being. Herbs must be combined with enhancing factors from other plants and nutritive substances to bring their full healing potential into the human realm. Then, they can help the body adjust its vibratory rate, and the body's vitality will follow with what is necessary to cure—which is simply an adjustment of the vibratory rate of the tissue to perform its balanced function."

—*A.S. Wheelwright, Private consultation, Houston, Texas, 1988*

Natural-health practitioners who master the use of these six formulas soon find that they enter into a new dimension of effectiveness in their work of assisting the body to restore the more optimal function that is inherent in its blueprint. For these reasons, Wheelwright is credited with ushering in a new era of herbal medicine.

The Six Systemic Bio-Command Formulas

The Bio-Command formulas are designed to combine with, enhance, and change (direct) the resulting influence of other Systemic herbal formulas (particularly Bio-Function formulas) on the targeted tissue in one of six ways:

1. **Activate** the tissue's inherent, normal function, **[#1 Activator]**
2. **Build** the tissue's integrity and functional abilities, **[#2 Builder]**
3. **Rid Bacteria** from the tissue and its extra-cellular matrix, **[#3 Bactrex]**
4. **Rid Fungal Involvement** from the tissue and its extra-cellular matrix, **[#4 Corrector]**
5. Help **Stabilize** mitosis (cellular reproduction and identity), and help the body correct errant DNA patterns (abnormal mutations), **[#5 Stabilizer]**
6. Increase the tissue's ability to **Heal** and regenerate **[#6 Healer]**.

Example: the Systemic Bio-Function formula K (Kidney) is designed to support the kidneys in *all* their inherent functions and activities including both anabolic and catabolic activities. When K (Kidney) is combined with Bio-Command #6 (Healer), the resulting therapeutic action is to increase the kidneys' specific ability to heal during that normal cycle of anabolic activity without disrupting other kidney activities including the acid-cycle processes. Thus, using K (Kidney) + #6 (Healer) together results in supporting the kidneys in *all* their cyclical activities with a specific, enhanced emphasis on soliciting and encouraging the tissue's healing and regeneration processes.

Bio-Commands Solve Herbal Medicine's Inherent Challenges

The capability to have one herbal formula *command* another herbal formula to perform specific actions solves the historic, key difficulties of practicing herbal medicine including:

1. Homeostasis (reduced effectiveness of herbal therapy over time),
2. Side-effects [*provings* (causing new symptoms) and detrimental effects],
3. Dissipation throughout the body instead of direct application to a particular tissue (how to deliver the herbal healing components to a specific tissue for a specific function, e.g. *targeting*),
4. Dosage effectiveness (*law of mass action* and the tissue's biochemical response),
5. Concerns regarding drug interactions,
6. Inventory limitations affecting therapeutic options.

Thus, the Wheelwright Healing System, pioneered by master herbalist A. Stuart Wheelwright, is a major breakthrough in both the effectiveness and practice of herbal medicine. How Wheelwright approached these historic challenges and used them to discover deeper principles of natural healing are the topics we'll discuss in this discourse.

The Wheelwright Viewpoint

While herbalists often cite Wheelwright's breakthroughs as "moving herbology into the 21st Century," and discuss the history and practice of herbology as "pre-Wheelwright and post-Wheelwright"; Wheelwright believed that his research was simply a natural extension, re-discovery, and validation of the hidden truths of natural healing. It was a marriage of the ancient wisdom of herbology found in the Chinese, Aruvedic, and Native American traditions (both North and

Wheelwright charts the sclera of a patient, explains the constitutional predispositions to illness, and correlates that overview to the person's current symptom picture.

South), with the modern science of quantum physics whereby the bio-energetic patterns of herbal combinations are matched with the archetypal, bio-energetic signatures of individual tissues.

"The causes of symptoms reside as resonance-disturbances in the tissue and are most often the result of bio-energetic congestion followed by physical congestion of lymph and blood followed by degeneration of tissue integrity."

—*A.S. Wheelwright, Lecture, Dallas, Texas, 1988*

To Wheelwright, plants (herbs) were the proper and appropriate medicines for the human being, and that the efficient design and combination of herbal formulas opened a new door into the effectiveness of herbal healing—one that could surpass the 'current deviation' of drug medicine for maintaining the health and vitality of the human being. He saw his work as the next step in exemplifying why herbs—with their inherent 'human-compatible' bio-energetic matrices—automatically became the vehicle for profound healing thus proving that herbal combinations were "The True Medicine" for the ailing human condition.

Wheelwright's Historic Research

To fully understand the applications of the Bio-Command formulas, it's important to understand how Wheelwright approached herbology and constructed, earlier in his career, the Bio-Function formulas—the primary formulas that the Bio-Commands direct.

Here-to-fore Un-thought-of. Wheelwright's research brought a nutritional depth, an herbal wisdom, and a progressive quantum-physics viewpoint that literally moved natural healing into an area of precision seldom, if ever before, attained. His resulting formulas increased the breadth and depth of herbal, nutritional healing into a system that could expand to keep pace with the new and ever-increasing ways humanity endeavors to destroy health. The unique and comprehensive factors that he applied to a single formulation include:

1. Herbal polarization [the use of herbs and nutrient factors that are compatible with the formula's direction—stimulation, tonification, or sedation, or to provide a balancing or drainage[2] factor.

2. Herbal enzymators for specific vitamins, minerals, and amino acids for greater assimilation and utilization by the cells.

3. Brazilian herbs (known for their pristine vitality and nascent qualities).

4. Bio-energetically 'tuning' the formula to a specific tissue or organ system, e.g. matching the formula's resonance to the tissue's resonance pattern.

5. Properly combining herbs synergistically to remove unwanted side effects while simultaneously enhancing the benefits.

6. Use of cellular identity factors (nucleo-protein structures that are the primal blueprints of cellular structure and function), when applicable.

Wheelwright catalogued physical substances according to their bio-energetic resonance patterns. He knew that energy structures— organized patterns of energy—define matter, and that health is first determined in the bio-energetic blueprint and resonance of a person.

Generally speaking, his research into the "signatures of substance" began in his private laboratory near Ogden, Utah. He catalogued matter that was organized by "life" by first taking an amount of desiccated substance (herb, mineral, vitamin, amino acid, or tissue, etc.) and adding it to a beaker of triple-distilled water. He then measured the change in the water's surface tension and viewed the results on an oscilloscope. From the sine wave that resulted, he calibrated a unique series of numbers that identified the bio-energetic matrix of the test-substance based on the height, breadth, and depth of the sine wave. Wheelwright's

---

[2] Drainage — assistance for the body's detoxification pathways (lymphatic, hepatic, renal) so that toxins and waste products can leave the body without congesting or obstructing the eliminative routes and result in aggravation of symptoms or cause new symptoms as the detoxification effort seeks other outlets (skin, lungs).

pet name for his lab equipment was the "biosynsizer." (Historical Note: When Wheelwright was in junior high school, his lab at home was recognized as one of the most advanced private labs in the Western United States).

Using one, definitive ellipsoid cycle portrayed on the scope, Wheelwright viewed it as one segment of a helix[3]. A cross section of the ellipsoid taken at the apex rendered a circle of which the diameter is the breadth of the bioforce. From this circle, Wheelwright derived three key 'signatures'. He catalogued the '*bio-valence*' as the radius (the distance from the hub to the perimeter); the '*quantum*' of the bio-force as the arc of the circle; and the '*bond*' which is the number of electron shells formed around the line of force. Wheelwright used these three calculations in determining the components of his formulations. With these numeric signatures, he endeavored to find the right 'balance' of ingredients that would facilitate a similar resonance field that the body could use, in addition to the traditional herbal components, for restoration of health.

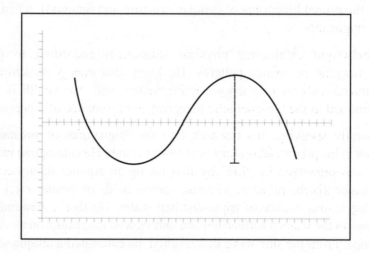

One of his calculations—the *bio-valence*—is the unique "resonance pattern" or "signature" of the substance that he most often referred to. Thus to Wheelwright, and in the modern day applications of his research, the plant, pimiento, is 1582 bvw (*bio-valence wheelwright*),

---

[3] Helix — a three-dimensional curve with a central axis and a steadily increasing, steadily decreasing, or constant circumference; spiral.

a healthy kidney is 16,842 *bvw*; the frontal lobe of the brain is 1,246,826 *bvw*; the herb chamomile is 624 *bvw*; the element, calcium, is 288 bvw, and so forth; with each physical substance resonating with a unique, characteristic frequency.

Summary Point
Wheelwright discovered how to measure the definitive life energies (bio-energetic resonance patterns) of life forms.

Wheelwright's theory was based on the fact that life structures are built on fundamental archetypal patterns—all variations on mathematical themes. He believed that herbs and nutriments could be combined and constructed to more effectively relate to a tissue, and that a deep secret of herbal healing would emerge in that the traditional herbs—historically known to help the body heal a specific tissue (liver, kidneys, etc.)—would have some mathematical component directly related to that tissue's bio-energetic signature pattern.

His first challenge was that, according to his calculations, the plant frequencies were categorically, vibrationally much lower than human tissue frequencies. His initial research was to apply the concept of "octaves". More specifically, it was an attempt to assume that the body could pull higher frequencies off the resonance pattern as long as it was in the same "key" as the tissue. Thus, if a plant resonated to 512 bvw, then it might affect a tissue whose resonance pattern was 16,384 (two numbers that share a mathematical sequence involving 2, 4, 8, 64, 128, 256). This theory quickly failed because not every tissue's measured resonance fell into a neat pattern of numbers, nor did the therapeutic herbs.

The breakthrough came when Wheelwright mixed an herbal combination of three herbs. He was experimenting on how to combine relaxing herbs into a formula that would not be sedating to the mind. He was seeking the ability to relax muscles and relieve tensions without impairing mental function with drowsiness. He selected the herbs catnip and chamomile as the relaxants, and boldo as a liver stimulant that would keep the metabolism active. The resulting formula showed good promise and was shared with John Christopher who also reported that the formula had some of the desired effect. [Note: years later this initial research would be perfected in the Nc (Nerve calm) formula which is based on a Brazilian herbal matrix with 15 ingredients.]

Wheelwright put the combination of the three herbs (after they had been ground together into a homogenous mixture) into his *biosynsizer* and was astounded to find that the resulting frequency pattern was much greater than the average or even sum total of the individual herbs. Now he found a way to have the plants 'talk' the same language as the body. It was in the proper combination rather than in their individual use. This launched Wheelwright's research for many years to come. He became a master jigsaw-puzzle assembler, mixing and matching herbs, vitamins, minerals, cellular identity factors, fatty acids, nucleo-proteins, and other nutritional factors to create masterpiece formulations that speak directly to the targeted tissue frequency and provide the fundamental components for healing and rejuvenation of the tissue's integrity. [Dr. Timothy Kuss provides an example of Wheelwright's formula design technique in his book, *A Guidebook to Clinical Nutrition for the Health Professional*, available at www.apple-a-daypress.com]

Summary Point
Wheelwright documented herbal synergism - that there is a "plus element" when compatible herbs are properly combined.

Example: How Wheelwright constructed an Herbal Formulation.

So, taking the Systemic H (Heart) formula for a specific example, Wheelwright started with the bio-energetic signature of the heart (72,909 *bvw*) and then looked at how herbs and nutritive factors could combine to 'create' or become 'tuned' to that frequency. To that effect, he assembled known nutritional factors and herbs and blended them in different combinations and proportions until they came together to support the heart.

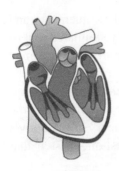 Wheelwright would often construct separate components or modules and then combine them with specific herbs to build the formula matrix— literally a three-dimensional jigsaw puzzle process of synergistic trial-and-error. More specifically, he knew that the H (Heart) formula needed an amino acid matrix to support the tissue integrity of the heart muscle and so he found that a triad of pheny-lalanine, l-carnitine, and tyrosine proved to be the most appropriate. After weeks of testing, he found that the mineral matrix would be based on a triad of calcium, potassium, and chromium with the supporting magnesium inherent in the herbal base.

As he worked, the B-vitamin lipids, choline and inositol, showed promise and so lecithin became a formula factor. The herbal matrix was assembled from hawthorn, tayuya, sete sangrias, and woodruff—an unusual combination of North and South American herbs. Vitamin cata-lysts, essential to the heart, were proportioned into a matrix of B-1, B-2, Niacin, B-6, Biotin, and Folic acid combined with appropriate herbs. The primal, healing, restorative cellular identity matrix was constructed with ingredients for the heart, thymus, and spleen making a triad of the basic blueprint information to support the longevity of the tissue and bio-energetic system.

In his research, Wheelwright found that not just the ingredients, but also the *proportion* of ingredients was critical. To make a truly effective formula meant not only finding the compatible ingredients for syner-gistic expansion of the resonance field, but even more importantly, finding the exact amounts in ratio to each other. This often meant that expensive ingredients needed to be of significant amounts, whereas the tendency in the herbal industry was to formulate by allowing only a token amount of the rare and expensive ingredients. Further, free form amino acids and other nutritive ingredients are quite costly compared to bales of herbs. Wheelwright struggled to provide formulas to the marketplace that ended up costing three to thirty times more to make. Toward the end of his life, his son, Stuart, Jr. helped with this by procuring and warehousing the raw materials in large quantities and becoming a supplier of rare herbs to the wholesale marketplace.

Once the ingredients were properly proportioned, sequenced, and combined, and the bio-energetic resonance accurately simulated that of the heart tissue, Wheelwright looked at the *bond* of the combined formula. If it exceeded the tissue's innate resonance pattern, then he knew that the formula had enough bio-energy to elicit the body's cooperation in the repair and restoration of the tissue. He theorized that the additional electrons provided an "informed refreshment" of the body's ch'i thus helping to dispel the bio-energetic congestion—a step that must occur for the true and deep healing to occur.

Summary Point
Wheelwright discovered that properly combined herbs, tuned to the life energies of human organs, formed a matrix that could attract additional energy.

In the last five years of Wheelwright's life, he re-worked his formulas to increase the *bond* ratings. He adjusted the ratios of ingredients, often adding or removing an ingredient to fine-tune the formula so that it could attract additional electron shells. When the bond energy exceeded his equipment's calibration, he labeled the formula an 'infinity' (∞) formula. This additional energy, once organized by the life-pattern of the tissue and supplied by the formula, contributed to both the power and gentleness of the formula allowing the nutrition to be a neutral, balanced beacon for the body to use as a pattern in its healing endeavor.

Wheelwright's research took him all over the world. He sought out the healers and 'barefoot' doctors in the remote corners of the globe and in this process spanning 40-years, he logged over 3.5 million air miles. From the jungles of the Philippeans to the mountains of Africa; from the rivers feeding the Amazon, to the headwaters of the Nile; from the back trails of China and the then-free Tibet, to the windswept islands of Scotland; Wheelwright sought out the herbs that had a healing tradition.

Nascent Vitality. It was in Brazil that he found many herbs with the innate vitality he sought. He understood that most of the Earth's plants were 'founded' in the Amazon watershed because that region was not covered with ice during the last ice age. There he found the plants that are the ancestors of the Earth's flora, and there he calibrated his calculations based on the vitality of the nascent plants in their pristine environment. While in Brazil, he established the responsible cultivation of herbs for use in his formulas so the rain forests would not be sacrificed to provide the healing components for a hugely populated world.

As Wheelwright's research progressed, he found that most of the herb formulas available for public consumption were incomplete. Many had good ingredients, some in good proportions; but they lacked the completing factors that would facilitate a truly deep healing of the tissue's integrity and function. He portrayed these formulas, two-dimensionally as a wheel with gaps and an incomplete rim.

INCOMPLETE FORMULAS

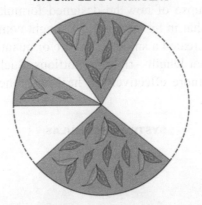

INCOMPLETE FORMULAS LACK IN CERTAIN CRITICAL ELEMENTS

Wheelwright also found that a few popular formulas had a good array of ingredients, but they were improperly balanced in that they did not adhere to the principles of herbal ionization or had improper proportions. Thus they had incompatible components that inhibited the expression of the body's ability to restore integrity and function. He depicted such formulas like this.

IMBALANCED FORMULAS

IMBALANCED FORMULAS OFTEN COMBINE INCOMPATIBLE ELEMENTS

In showing a glimpse of how he designed formulas, he portrayed a wheel and stated that in his research, he sought combinations that had no gaps and thus created a smooth rim (arc or quantum), and that they had spokes of equal length—right proportions. Such a formula would 'move' the body more effectively to heal and renew the tissue with nutritive elements.

SYSTEMIC FORMULAS

SYSTEMIC FORMULAS RESONATE WITH THE VITAL FORCES OF THE BODY SYSTEMS

In ancient times, the secret art of Wheel-wrighting (wheel making) was based on geometry: how many spokes to use and where to place them into the rim. A correctly made wheel worked well and was strong because the vibrations of its turning did not weaken its structure; whereas a poorly made wheel vibrated discordantly and soon fell apart. True to his name, Wheelwright practiced the art of wheel making so the body's inner turnings could spiral into greater health.

To construct his formulas, Wheelwright made use of numerous nutrients and catalysts. This diagram shows the many components that he made available to the body for a multi-dimensional healing effort.

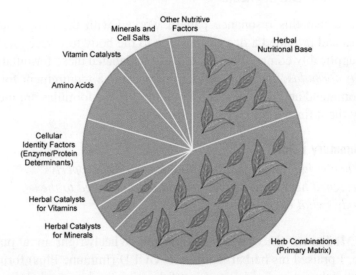

SYSTEMIC BIO-FUNCTION FORMULA MATRIX

Other Nutritive Factors

Minerals and Cell Salts

Vitamin Catalysts

Herbal Nutritional Base

Amino Acids

Cellular Identity Factors (Enzyme/Protein Determinants)

Herbal Catalysts for Vitamins

Herbal Catalysts for Minerals

Herb Combinations (Primary Matrix)

Wheelwright's research was actually based on a three dimensional model and his formula constructions were, in his words, assembled like the five- and six-sided cells of a soccer ball with each ingredient being a cell that held the soccer ball together. Thus his formula matrix was actually a sphere rather than a circle.

Once the sphere could 'spin', meaning that it properly resonated with the numeric values of the bio-energetic signature of the targeted tissue, Wheelwright found that the nutritive combination attracted more *bond*—additional electron shells. This additional energy was an extension of the archetypal energy pattern established by the compatible ingredients. He called this additional energy "the infinite vitality of the formula" and believed that it contributed, in a small way, to the flow of ch'i around and through the body, or rather that it supported the tissue resonance at a much deeper level, and from this resonance the body's ch'i gains flow and momentum.

He found that this resonance pattern worked with the body's subtle energies and provided a deeper message to the body to correct discord in the applicably compatible tissue. Thus, he labeled these formulations "*infinity formulas*," and this refinement became a requirement for the Bio-Command and Bio-Function formulas. [These formulas are identified by the infinity symbol (∞) on the label.]

Summary Point
Wheelwright found that the bio-energetics of properly-designed herbal/nutritional formulas contributed to the body's vital energies.

True Medicine. Once when introducing Wheelwright in a public lecture, I praised his herbal 'antibiotic' GOLD (Immune Plus) formula as being "almost as good as a powerful antibiotic drug for helping the body overcome bacterial infection—without the side effects!" Wheelwright immediately took issue with my viewpoint and exclaimed, "Herbs are far superior to drugs when properly combined," and proceeded to lecture on the healing power of herbs and the damaging, suppressive, fundamental shortsightedness of drugs. He would tolerate no compromise of the fundamental position that in Nature's design, herbs are the appropriate and true medicine for the human being.

"Herbs are God's medicines. They exist in Nature in a specific relationship to humans. There are herbs—be they grasses, roots, barks, flowers, stems, or leaves, or growths on plants—to help

the body cure every malady. The healing is not in the herb, it is in the body. The herbal matrix elicits the body's healing mechanism and serves as a reminder to the body to return to its optimal vibratory rate."

—A.S. Wheelwright, Lecture, Austin, Texas, 1987

Now let's take the pinnacle of Wheelwright's work—the Bio-Command Formulas—and examine them to understand what the Wheelwright Legacy is, and how to apply it in clinical practice.

Using the Bio-Command formulas is amazingly simple. But to reach that simplicity, we must first understand some key components of Wheelwright's research and thus, inadvertently in that process, become more skilled in the philosophy of natural healing.

Bio-Command Formulas Increase Results

In their most simple practice and most basic application, the Bio-Command formulas magnify the effectiveness of the accompanying Bio-Function formula two to four times, so many practitioners use Bio-Commands to hasten the beneficial actions of their therapeutic programs.

> **PRACTICE TIP:** Always select a Bio-Command formula to accompany the Bio-Function formula that addresses, by your analysis, the body's key or pivotal tissue i.e. the weakest tissue or the point of leverage that, when improved, your patient's health will improve. Thus, if you are designing a hypoglycemic support program and are using the following formulas: Ps (Pancreas-s), Ga (Adrenal), Gf (Thyroid) and L (Liver); and you have determined that the thyroid gland is the weakest link, use the Bio-Command formula #1 (Activator) with the Gf (Thyroid) to help elicit more rapid cooperation in the metabolically stabilizing thyroid function.

Wheelwright based this opinion on the improvement in tissue vitality as measured bio-energetically at two-hour intervals for twelve hours after taking the Bio-Command formula with the Bio-Function formula as compared to taking the Bio-Function formula without the Bio-

Command. The baseline was the tissue vitality ratings measured a day before taking the herbal supplements.

Herbs Elicit Innate Healing. Herbal healing depends on the body's cooperation. Wheelwright also found that the extent of the increased performance of a Bio-Command formula was unique to the individual patient and the circumstances of the tissue congestion. Thus a person with poor vitality did not have as great of an initial bio-energetic response as one who was in better overall health; but with a little time, even the lower vitalities would gain bio-energetic strength as a result of the herbal therapy. [Practitioners often find success in advanced, chronic and degenerative cases with Wheelwright's formulas (where other formulas have failed) because of their ability to re-establish the bio-energetic matrix as a source for the body to effect the necessary corrections.]

Wheelwright then determined that the vitality increase was partially governed by the assistance of the body's own, innate healing energies as they responded to the resonance of the herbal combination and so it was not solely a function of the herbal formulas applied. Thus he proved that the formulas could help elicit the body's own healing response in addition to simply providing bio-energetic and biochemical elements.

"The herbal matrix of my formulas helps the body re-organize its bio-energetic pattern and serves as a catalyst to re-structure the errant, confused, distorted energy pattern of an ailing tissue. They enliven and enhance the body's original, optimal pattern and serve as a beacon for the body's healing processes to follow."

—A.S. Wheelwright, *Private Conversation with Jack Tips, 1989*

Example: Bio-Energetic Increase from Systemic Herbal Matrix

A 42 year-old woman, presenting a history of Non-Hodgkin's Lymphoma (spleen not removed) remised with chemotherapy/radiation treatment, sought nutritional help for the resulting loss of vitality and impaired mental clarity. Since the drug intervention, she had "never regained her energy, caught every cold, and never stabilized her white blood count." Prior to consulting with Wheelwright, she had worked with an acupuncturist (herbalist/nutritionist) to detoxify, support the liver, cleanse the lymphatic system, and rebuild her health nutritionally. Wheelwright took her case, charted her sclera[4] and determined that her spleen was "the ball and chain" dragging her energy down. An accompanying acupuncturist independently confirmed that the spleen was an area of great concern.

On Day One, Wheelwright measured her spleen energy every two hours for six measurements during his consulting and lecture schedule, and recorded her baseline spleen vitality to be in the range of 861-863 *bvw* (*bio-valence wheelwright*). This was between three and four times less than the optimal range. On Day Two the patient took 1 S (Spleen) capsule at 2 hour intervals. On Day Three, the patient took 1 S (Spleen) + 1 #2 (Builder) at 2-hour increments. After the 3 days of testing, the patient continued taking 2 S (Spleen) + 1 #2 (Builder) twice a day for 40 days.

- *Tissue measured: Spleen*
- *Formulas applied: 1 capsule S (Spleen), 1 capsule #2 (Builder) as specified*
- *Patient: Weakened vitality, 13-months after treatment for Non-Hodgkin's Lymphoma*
- *Baseline Spleen Vitality: 862 bvw (bio-valence-wheelwright)*
- *Target Spleen Vitality after 40 days treatment: 28,866 bvw.*

Vitality (Bio-energetic) Reading	2 hr	4hr	6 hr	8 hr	10 hr	12 hr
Before herbal support spleen vitality =	862	862	862	863	861	861
After 1 S (Spleen)	11684	11883	11886	11885	11885	11885
After 1 S (Spleen) + 1 #2 (Builder)	26104	26139	26268	26199	26466	27006

---

[4] Sclera — the white of the eyes. Wheelwright discovered and developed the art and science of Sclerology—the study of the red lines in the whites of the eyes for their reflexive portraits of constitutional and acquired stress. More information at www.sclerology-institute.org

The patient, S. Brady, best reports the results: *"Within the first day I noticed an improved energy as I did not fade in the afternoon. By the end of the first week, I felt a strong, sustained fortitude and had a more positive outlook than I'd had in over five years. I found I was able to exercise and plan on evening activities. This continued for the duration of the program and continued after I stopped the herbal supplementation."*

Wheelwright found that by introducing a greater bio-energetic vitality to the tissue as well as the herbal biochemical elements—both inherent in his Systemic formulas—that the tissue could and would respond faster and more thoroughly to effect the necessary adjustments to achieve a more optimal function.

Interpretation: After one capsule of S (Spleen), the spleen energy was significantly enhanced. That alone would, over the course of perhaps 72-days, restore the patient to more optimal spleen health. With the first dose of S (Spleen) + #2 (Builder), the spleen bio-energetics more than doubled showing that the addition of the Bio-Command formula enhanced the S (Spleen) Bio-Function formula in the direction it needed most, and thus hastened results. Once the proper bio-energetic matrix was in place via the herbal therapy, the body was provided a beacon to follow, one that lead to recovery of the tissue over a short period of time.

"The herbs, once properly combined and 'tuned' to the tissue's optimal resonance pattern, serve as a guide or beacon to encourage the tissue to re-organize or throw off the congestion that inhibits its proper function and restore itself to the best vitality it can achieve. It's a reminder, a wake-up call, to return to better health."

— A.S. Wheelwright, Austin, Texas, 1987

Obvious Question. Occasionally, a practitioner asks, "Since, for example, the Bio-Command formulas #1 (Activator) increases the effectiveness of a Bio-Function formula such as Gf (Thyroid) two to four times, why didn't Wheelwright simply put a little of it in the Gf (Thyroid) formula and have a better overall formula?"

The answer, obvious when contemplated, is that not every thyroid condition needs "*activation*." The Gf (Thyroid) formula is a most excellent formula all by itself. But it takes the doctor's knowledge, evaluation, and insights in understanding the patient's case, to determine if the thyroid needs an 'activating' influence instead of a '*building*' or '*healing*' influence.

Serendipitous Increase in Effectiveness. The increased effectiveness that the Bio-Command formulas add to an herbal program was not Wheelwright's original intent in designing the Bio-Command formulas! His initial work focused on two applications: 1) providing the ability to apply the balanced, neutral, healing factors of a Bio-Function formula toward a specific directive, as well as 2) provide a system that works around the limitations of homeostasis (this will be discussed in the next section) to allow the body a longer more thorough healing response. As often happens in quantum physics, there is a synergistic effect of geometric proportion. It was a most pleasant surprise to find that an increase in effectiveness automatically accompanied the newly found ability to direct the tissue in a specific, inherent process.

When Wheelwright spoke of the blessing of increased effectiveness resulting from his Bio-Command research, his eyes would literally sparkle with the awe and amazement of the oneness and transcendence of life; coupled with the humility that he was the vehicle for these 'little elements of truth'.

Bio-Command Formula Compatibility With Other Systemic Formulas

Bio-Commands are designed to automatically combine with other Systemic formulas, particularly the Bio-Function formulas, but they also serve other categories of formulas such as the Bio-Challenge and Chinese Five-Element Formulas that comprise Systemic Formulas, Inc.'s catalog of offerings.

Neutral, Nourishing Impact. Because Wheelwright 'tuned' his Bio Function formulas to the inherent 'neutral' vibratory rate of the targeted tissue—meaning generally that they generally do not focus on either over-stimulation or over-sedation of the tissue, but rather serve to nourish the tissue and support the archetypal resonance—the herb-derived bio-energetic pattern automatically harmonizes with the body-tissue's optimal, functional vibrational key (innate resonance); thus compatibility with other Systemic Formulas naturally occurred. [More on this in the upcoming section: *"Allopathy, Homeopathy and the Balance Principle."*] Suffice it here to point out that virtually all of Wheelwright's formulas are compatible with each other with no harm being done due to the combined presence of any of the Systemic formulas.

> **PRACTICE TIP:** There is a theoretical exception to the 'all compatibility rule' that occurred when Wheelwright made his famous liver formulas—L (Liver) and Ls (Liver-S). In this instance, Wheelwright intended that the formulas be used at separate times of the day. By common practice, the Ls (Liver-S) is often taken in the morning because its properties (based on herbal polarization) lean more toward the *stimulation* of liver function, and then the L (Liver) is taken in the evening because its inherent properties lean more toward the *building* function. Because of the unique and very complex activities of the liver, Wheelwright's 'neutral' tissue support occurs when both formulas are used in a program at separate times. If someone ingested both formulas together, they do not 'cancel each other out' as some have erroneously surmised. They are still effective in improving liver function as verified in clinical practice. However, the greatest effectiveness comes from separating the formulas and allowing each to have its own time of influence. [More information on Wheelwright's liver research is in the book: *The Healing Triad—Your Liver, Your Lifeline* available at www.apple-a-daypress.com.]

Tissue vs. Function. Wheelwright often distinguished between a tissue's inherent integrity and the function of that tissue in action. For example, to him there was, 1) the kidney tissue which included the extra-cellular matrix and integrity (vitality) of its cells; and 2) the nephron, glomerulus, and tubule cells' ability to perform their functions such as filtering the blood, absorbing vitamin D, adjusting pH, excreting wastes, salt conservation and reabsorption, etc. If an herbal formulation tended toward the anabolic ionization, then the formula leaned toward *building* the inherent vitality and collagen of the tissue itself. If a formula tended toward the catabolic ionization, then it would encourage improved *function* of that tissue in its inherent activities.

Multiplicity of Research. Because of his continuous research and experimentation, Wheelwright designed more than one formula for a specific tissue. In many ways, the multiple formulas are interchangeable for that tissue and either one will bring good results. The practitioner cannot make a mistake in choosing one over the other, yet there are nuances that can make one formula more appropriate at a given time. For more information on the Bio-Function formulas and differentiations between seemingly redundant formulas, see Appendix A.

For an example of Bio-Command enhancement, to design a systemic herbal program to help the body correct a weak digestion and restore the stomach's ability to manufacture hydrochloric acid and pepsin, a practitioner would choose the formula D (Digestive). To hasten the results in this specific endeavor, the D (Digestive) formula can be combined with Bio-Command #1 (Activator). Thus many practitioners consider the Bio-Commands to be a way to strengthen the healing impact of the accompanying formula and testify to the improved results they observe in clinical practice.

"Bio-Command formulas help deliver quicker corrective results two ways: 1) They increase the effective-action of the accompanying Bio-Function formula by providing additional directive components, and 2) they increase the targeted tissue's receptivity to the healing influence of the herbal factors—both biochemically and bio-energetically. These two actions bring profound healing results when properly applied."

— A.S. Wheelwright, Practitioner's Meeting, Ogden, UT, 1988

Wheelwright researched the inherent healing factors in herbs and applied them according to their pH, ionization potentials, enzymes, ionic minerals, polysaccharides, and nucleo-proteins as well as how they combined with other herbs to create new 'frequencies' in their bio-energetic patterns. As already stated, he designed the Bio-Command formulas to be compatible with his other non-Bio-Command formulas, and to encourage the targeted tissue to become more receptive to the nourishment being provided.

"Receptivity of the targeted tissue's cells to the herbal healing is a multi-faceted, cooperative endeavor. I have succeeded in creating superior healing formulas by cooperating with the body's innate healing faculties by first learning how to deliver the herbal healing factors to the targeted tissue with the help of compatible energy-signatures as well as RNA-DNA identity factors that restore the deep damage and loss of integrity.

Further, the ionization potential of the herbs must be balanced and made compatible with what the tissue needs—either anionic (building), or cationic (cleansing) component .... or both to modify a tendency to cause unnecessary aggravation. Occasionally, a poly-ionic (tonic) such as yarrow or ginseng is called for in a formula. This compatibility is further enhanced by the availability of enzymes, saccharide complexes, vitamin co-factors, alkaloids, nucleo-proteins and mineral components of the herb combinations or the formula itself."

— *A.S. Wheelwright, 1986, Conversation with Practitioners, St. Petersburg, FL*

Cellular Assimilation. Encouraging the target tissue to become more receptive to the healing information of the herbs is called "cellular receptivity." Wheelwright used to say, *"It's not what you eat, it's what you digest, assimilate, and utilize that sets the standard of your nutrition."* He was perpetually pre-occupied with cellular receptivity and assimilation throughout his research and endeavored, with each formula he designed, to make the herb's healing components readily acceptable to the tissue. He found that certain mineral and enzyme components could be included in a formula to enhance cellular assimilation of the herbal nutrition.

Bio-Command Formulas Help Direct The Healing Action of Other Herbal Formulas in Clinical Practice

Once practitioners select a Bio-Function Formula (named for the tissue it supports such as Adrenal, Brain, Kidney, Lung, Nerve, Pancreas, Pituitary, Spleen, Thyroid, etc.) they have the option of adding a Bio-Command formula to accomplish a more specific purpose.

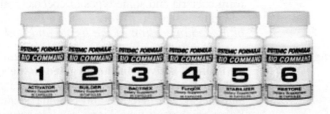

Here is a chart to help understand the basic applications of the Bio-Command Formulas.

Bio Command Formula	General Purpose & Additional Information
#1 (Activator)	**Increases the targeted tissue's assimilation of herbal nutrition. Stimulates the tissue's inherent active functions during the tissue's active cycle.** Enhances the tissue's ability to activate its chief function by increasing its receptivity to balancing influences of the Bio-Function formula. Stimulates sluggish tissue to perform optimally, but does not over stimulate. Optimizes the activity of the 6.2 - 6.9 pH-cycle activities. Supports the hypothalamic communication of information to the brain. *Works within the overall balanced operation of the tissue!*
#2 (Builder)	**Helps relax the targeted tissue and enhance its inherent re-building, self-maintenance processes during the tissue's restful, re-construction cycle.** Enhances the tissue's receptivity to the building components of the body and the Bio-Function formula's nutrition. Stimulates more effective rebuilding of collagen within the Bio-Function formula's bio-energetic matrix. Optimizes the building activity of the more alkaline 7.1 - 7.59 pH-cycle activities. *Works within the overall balanced operation of the tissue!*

#3 (Bactrex)   **Assists and stimulates the immune system's anti-bacterial activity in the targeted tissue's extra-cellular matrix.** May be used by itself as a systemic anti-bacterial, anti-infective, anti-mycotic[5], immune-supporting agent. Enhances the anti-bacterial activity in the tissue targeted by the Bio-Function formula. Helps restore normal immune function after the suppressive and deranging action of antibiotic use. Can interfere with the reproduction of some rod-form bacteria and some types of coccus (both gram + and gram –) bacteria. *Works within the overall balanced operation of the tissue and body!*

#4 (FungDx)   **Assists and stimulates the immune system's anti-fungal activity in the targeted tissue's extra-cellular matrix.** May be used by itself as a systemic anti-fungal, anti-mycotic, anti-candida agent. Enhances the anti-fungal, anti-candida activity in the tissue targeted by the Bio-Function formula. Enhances the anti-viral, anti-streptococcus and anti-staphylococcus response. May actually kill some forms of fungus. Works via the lymph as well as the bloodstream. *Works within the overall balanced operation of the body!*

#5 (Stabilizer)   **Helps the targeted tissue resist abnormal cellular mitosis, errant biogenic cellular proliferations, and DNA-altering viral activity, thus helping the tissue's cells retain their inherent cellular identity.** It helps strengthen the cells innate resistance to abnormal developments such as anaerobic fermenta-tions, mycosis, and rapid proliferations. Stimulates proper cellular reproduction, thus helps prevent cellular, genetic degeneration (loss of telomeres). Increases cellular immunity regarding abnormal cellular development. Helps cells resist any degenera-tive process. Helps re-establish cellular integrity. *Works within the overall balanced operation of the tissue!*

#6 (Restore)   **Helps trigger and accelerate the repair of damaged tissue during its inherent healing (deep rest) cycle.** Can be used by itself as a systemic healing agent. Promotes the formation of the alkaline pH necessary for healing. Enhances the body's

---

[5] Mycotic — from the word mycosis: any disease caused by a fungus.

response to trauma and injury. Assists in the repair of collagen and soft tissue. Helps the body repair the effects of free-radical damage. *Works within the overall balanced operation of the tissue.*

Bio-Command Thought Process. With this understanding, practitioners have the ability to add a Bio-Command formula if and when they desire its influence. Thus, the thought-process is often as simple as this. If you:

- want to have the thyroid be less sluggish, you can add the #1 (Activator) to the Gf (Thyroid) formula.
- choose to rebuild the liver because of the patient's history of excessive alcohol consumption, you can add the #2 (Builder) with the two Liver formulas (L and Ls).
- determine that there is a chronic, bacterial infection affecting the spleen and lymphatic system, add the #3 (Bactrex) to the S (Spleen) formula.
- need to focus on a fungal involvement in the prostate, combine the #4 (FungDx) with the Mpc (Prostata Corrector) formula.
- are concerned about abnormal cellular development in the uterus, you can apply the #5 (Stabilizer) with the F+ (Female) formula.
- want to help the body heal the adrenal glands after a period of severe stress, burn, or trauma; you'll combine the #6 (Healer) with the Ga (Adrenal) formula.

So, it's quite simple to couple a Bio-Command formula to the primary tissue support formula (Bio-Function) and enhance the results of any Systemic program. Many practitioners like to run a sequence of Bio-Command formulas at two-week intervals to support a tissue in different processes. For example, an adrenal support program could be:

Adrenal support program

Days 1-14 . . . . 2 Ga (Adrenal) + 1 #6 (Healer), *bid,* then

Days 15-28 . . . 2 Ga (Adrenal) + 1 #2 (Builder), *bid,,* then

Days 29-42 . . . 2 Ga (Adrenal) + 1 #1 (Activator), *bid.*

Such a cycle is compatible with Wheelwright's position that it often takes 40-days to effect a new stability in a tissue's foundational integrity. Thus many practitioners will use a Bio-Function formula for six weeks, introducing different Bio-Command formulas that also serve to avoid the limiting effects of homeostasis (as we will soon discuss).

There is much more we can do with the Bio-Command formulas, and the best part is this: once we understand the philosophy of the Bio-Command Formulas, it's very simple to know when and what to use.

Discourse 2:
The Six Challenges That Limit Herbal Medicine's Effectiveness and Wheelwright's Solutions

To further understand the potentials of using the Bio-Command formulas, we must understand some of the inherent shortcomings of herbal medicine as it has been practiced over the past centuries and is still being practiced today. In the overview at the beginning of this book, six shortcomings were cited. Let's examine these issues and advance our knowledge and applications of the Systemic Bio-Command Formulas.

Challenge #1: Homeostasis and The Bio-Command Formulas

One reason Wheelwright made the Bio-Command formulas was to breach the limitations of the "homeostasis principle" and still cooperate with the laws of natural healing.

The Bio-Commands allow the herbal therapy to 'stay alive' and actively impact the improvement process, encouraging the body to participate in the therapeutic mode much longer than with conventional herbal therapies. This results in a more rapid and thorough healing response.

We must keep in mind that Wheelwright brought forth a new dimension in the healing potentials of herbs and thus created a new system of herbology that far exceeds what most people know as herbology today. [More information on Wheelwright's herbal philosophy is in the books "*The Healing Triad: Your Liver—Your Lifeline*" (Tips, 1993), and in "*Guidebook To Clinical Nutrition For The Health Professional*" (Kuss, 1996.)]

Homeostasis: The Great Balancing Principle

Homeostasis is the body's great adaptation and balancing principle and it will use all its resources to maintain the essential and necessary environment for life processes. The vital force of every living organism has an inherent self-preservation mechanism whose primary mission is "adapt and survive" also known as "homeostasis."

"Homeostasis is the dynamic force in the body that maintains metabolic equilibrium and balance—an innate wisdom that perpetuates adaptations necessary for survival, even at the expense of comfort. Its prime directive is 'adapt to survive' and gives little thought to the cost on the body's resources."

—*Tips, Discourses on Homeopathy, 1984*

"Homeostasis is a tendency to stability in the normal body states (internal environment) of the organism. It is achieved by a system of control mechanisms activated by negative feedback, for example a high level of carbon dioxide in extra-cellular fluid triggers increased pulmonary ventilation, which in turn causes a decrease in carbon dioxide concentration."

— *Medical Dictionary*

Homeostasis works on many levels within a human being. Here's a few examples. It makes countless minor adjustments to our bodies' chemistries to maintain proper blood elements and pH (acid/alkaline balance). It ensures that the calcium and glucose metabolic processes operate within established parameters. It automatically adjusts to the external environment with temperature adjustments, lacrimation, shivering, pupil dilation, perspiration, and so forth. Our bodies' energy, enzyme reactions, and defense (immune) systems are all founded on our innate vitality's ability to maintain homeostasis and thus maintain life.

In seeking to maintain homeostatic balance, the body's Vital Force can act aggressively, even violently, and initiate high fevers, severe coughs, vomiting, profuse sweats, powerful food cravings, and diarrhea. The greater the perceived threat, the more aggressive the Vital Force's homeostatic adjustment.

The Janus of Homeostasis. There are two sides to homeostasis. While it is fundamentally a beneficial influence that automatically protects our ability to adapt to our environment and stay alive, it can and will do this at the expense of tissue integrity. The bone-loss disease, osteoporosis, is one example. To maintain the homeostasis of the blood stream and its proper pH (slightly alkaline operating environment) in the presence of an overly acidic dietary pattern, the body will pull calcium ions out of the bones and place them in the bloodstream. Without the calcium ions in the bloodstream, the body would have died, so homeostasis did the right thing, but there is also the negative effect of its action—the resulting osteoporosis of de-calcified bones that break easily.

The Dimming of the Light

The body often slips into chronic symptoms through a "dimming of the light" process. What is meant by the phrase, "dimming of the light," is simply that the body will endeavor to 'make do' and adapt to a less than optimal functional state and then establish a new homeostasis at that sub-optimal level. If the light in your room were dimmed 10%, your eyes would adjust and get used to that level of light. Then with another 10% dimming, your eyes would compensate again. If this dimming/compensation activity continues, finally, without really noticing the process, the light would become too dim and the condition overtly noticed. This process is true of many of the body's symptoms.

Like the frog that jumps out of the soup pot's scalding water, but stays in the pot if the water is heated gradually to the boiling point; the human body adapts and compensates to little health issues and can continue to make small adaptations until they become advanced, chronic, degenerative diseases with debilitating symptoms.

Thus, the body may be experiencing a sub-optimal homeostasis with only the vague memory of optimal health. When the doctor/herbalist provides herbal therapies to correct that condition, the therapies have to help the body adjust and adapt to a more optimal homeostasis. During this time of change, the existing homeostasis can actually provide a resistance to the healing process.

Aggravations. Sometimes this resistance to change is called a "healing crisis," an "aggravation," a "Herxheimer reaction," or a "detoxification." The body and its homeostasis are so estranged from the optimal blueprint that it has allowed layer upon layer of compensated homeostasis. Further, the loss of tissue integrity of an organ or gland means that the body just doesn't have the wherewithal to reclaim health rapidly. The move to reclaim the optimal blueprint causes multiple body systems to resist the change in homeostasis.

Wheelwright wanted his formulas to work gently with the body to elicit the needed healing response without forcing it into reactions and resistances. He wanted his formulas to be guides and allies in the healing processes he believed were inherent in the body, and cooperate with the body's innate intelligence over the necessary period time. Thus his research became preoccupied with how to maintain herbal therapies long enough for the body to effect repair and allow the homeostatic status quotient to adapt without meeting the resistances that cause failure.

"No one knows how to heal your body better than your body. No doctor, no machine, no herbalist, no one. It's just that many people's bodies have temporarily forgotten how to heal, and their tissue integrity is too weak due to the loss of 'cellular identity' and collagen integrity to function at the level required to heal. Thus they stay stuck in a lower level of homeostasis. My formulas address this situation."

— A.S. Wheelwright, Kingwood, Texas 1986

Homeostasis minimizes both detrimental and beneficial effects.

Homeostasis minimizes the effects of both detrimental and beneficial activities because both of these activities can alter the current balance of the body's functions as they are being expressed at the present time. Thus homeostasis is a neutral force that applies to both good and bad influences in the body. Anything that causes radical changes (either good or bad) will come up against the homeostasis principle. Thus it can be both an ally and an adversary to the herbal nutritionist seeking to help a person improve their fundamental level of health.

> **PRACTICE TIP.** With homeostasis in mind, herbal healing can best adopt the "frog in the soup pot" technique of gently and gradually helping the body re-claim its more optimal health with small, consistent degrees of improvement. It serves the body best to gradually brighten the light so the adjustments are easily accepted. Starting with small doses of the herb formulas (i.e. one capsule twice a day) and gradually increasing the dosage over time (two weeks later, two capsules twice a day) is an effective technique that brings the most rewarding results.

"Healing is more gentle and powerful simultaneously when using the 'neutral' force. My formulas do not attempt to force sudden change on a tissue from a confrontational standpoint as is often done in traditional herbology as well as in allopathic drug-medicine. Instead, they provide the compatible, innate resonance of optimally healthy tissue—a renewal of the fundamental blueprint of health—and remind and guide the tissue to the best integrity and function it is capable of. Each day, each dose draws the tissue closer to the goal of its foundational health within the overall body system."

—A.S. Wheelwright, San Antonio, Texas, 1986

Negative Homeostasis. For further insight on homeostasis, let's consider the effects of ethanol on human metabolism. If alcohol is detrimental to the body, how do alcoholics get away with it for so long? Well, homeostasis is the answer. The body adapts to a steady diet of alcohol. Its metabolism adjusts to the burning of alcohol as a fuel and the liver harnesses nutritional resources to the reduction and processing of the alcohol and its toxic by-products. Homeostasis protects the life-processes and the body adapts. This is also why there are withdrawal symptoms when alcohol is stopped. The body no longer has what its adoptive-homeostasis has adapted it to have, and there is the pain and stress (such as *delirium tremens*) of changing the basic metabolic processes. [More on alcoholism and Systemic Formulas is in the book, *The Next Step To Greater Energy* (Tips, 1988) available as a web download at www.apple-a-daypress.com.]

Positive Homeostasis. Conversely, homeostasis also acts on the positive side of balance. Alcohol was a negative example because its excess causes severe side effects resulting from the body's struggle to adapt to it such as cirrhosis of the liver, brain damage (dementia), depression, and cardiovascular damage. But on the positive side, a therapy that is exceedingly beneficial to the body will also come up against homeostasis or the body's resistance to adapt to the new, beneficial influence. Thus, homeostasis will minimize a beneficial therapy when it's repeated enough to demand major changes if there are pockets of resistance to the move toward a higher vibratory rate.

Good health is a neutral balanced state of daily homeostatic corrections.

Major Alarm -100	Radical Reactions -75	Homeo-stasis -50	Good Health 0	Homeo-stasis +50	Radical Reactions +75	Major Alarm +100

Panaceas. The body's resistance to positive influences is the bane of people who perpetually seek 'the panacea'—the cure all. This is often seen when a marketing company introduces a "cure all" product. The testimonials flood in on how great the customers feel. However, if you check back with those people in three months, you'll find that the results are seldom lasting. They cannot stay in that exalted state of "feeling 20 years younger" because homeostasis acts and the body sets limits to how far the miracle-working product could push it; or the product itself went as far as it could and could not exert any more benefits due to lack of comprehensive support. At this point, people often stop using the 'miracle' product and start seeking the next one that promises to be a cure all. Or, they continue as 'die-hard users' and develop new symptoms called "provings" which occur due to the therapeutic action of the product which is continued too long, i.e. "too much of a good thing."

Provings and Side Shows. Developing new symptoms means that if the 'miracle product' was truly therapeutic, over time, it will start to cause symptoms as the body will have to adapt and compensate against the therapeutic agents. I observed this phenomenon first-hand with a patient who went to 'cloud nine' taking a blue green algae product. After continued use, the effects began to fade, and soon were replaced by symptoms including headaches, nasal discharge, joint aches and chronic fatigue. Instead of stopping the product and its excessively therapeutic action, the patient phoned the marketing company and was told to double the dose. Following this errant advice caused acute distress that, fortunately, caused the patient to become compliant and stop the supplement—an action that quickly brought a return to better health.

The point here is not that algae products are harmful. Quite the opposite as they are often beneficial as therapeutic agents, but not necessarily suited to frequent and continued use in every person. They are, in susceptible people, therapeutic to the point that daily use or excessive use is detrimental and the body must labor to adjust to them. This is not the 'cleansing reaction' fostered by a beneficial agent, but a reaction against the therapeutic components themselves. Thus for the patient cited above, algae is a medicine and should be used as such.

So with beneficial therapeutic agents, there is initially an improvement phase, then a phase of leveling out or 'diminishing returns', then if overuse continues, there will be detrimental side effects or an aggravation that occurs. If the therapeutic benefits 'level out' before there is complete restoration of optimal health, then the therapy fails to be curative.

"The use of the neutral force in herbal healing means that the herbal formula is not very likely to cause symptoms, even if used for extended periods of time. My formulas are powerful, yet have much less chance of causing aggravations and sideshows of extraneous symptoms because they are designed to 'bring the tissue home' rather than force a drastic change. People who are acutely sensitive and strongly resistant to healing can aggravate in any healing endeavor that helps adjust their vibratory rate. Fortunately, in herbal medicine, the dosage can easily be adjusted to a percentage of a capsule or a drop of a tincture or extract to allow the most gentle path to regain health."

—*A.S. Wheelwright, Lecture to practitioners, Austin, Texas 1988*

The Quest For Cure

Self-healing is inherent in the body's blueprint. If the therapy, whether it be drug or herb, does not restore health to the patient, then it fails to elicit a cure from the body and the patient must seek other assistance. But regardless of what doesn't work, the cure does exist and can be found, unless there is irreparable damage or inability to hold a higher resonance.

I often ask patients, "I see that you've been on blood pressure medication for two years. That's a long time to wait for it to cure, and the side effects are certainly a concern. When will this treatment bring a cure?"

The patient replies, "Oh, the medicine won't cure. It just keeps my blood pressure down as long as I'm taking it."

[Note: a loose definition of an *addiction* is that you have to keep taking something to get an effect.] In natural health, we must always seek the curative process, which is the restoration of health and the return of the body's ability to maintain its optimal health without the need to continue to take therapeutic agents.]

Self-limiting Formulas. Doc Wheelwright followed this rule and only made herbal therapeutic supplements that were self-limiting. But to accomplish this, he developed a system of being able to use the healing influence of therapeutic herbs for the required length of time to effect cure (sometimes as long as four or five months) without having homeostasis reduce their effectiveness. He did this two ways: 1) by creating tissue-frequency balanced formulas (Bio-Function), and 2) six formulas that change the tone and enhance an aspect of the Bio-Function formula without having to abandon it—the Bio-Command formulas.

The Bio-Command Solution To Homeostasis

As we've learned, the difficulty that herbology has with homeostasis is this: if the herbal therapy is too beneficial, the body will adapt and minimize its effectiveness. It's a simple law of diminishing returns. Eventually, using the same herbs over time will fail to act in bringing the body to a new plateau of more optimal health once the body establishes a homeostatic comfort zone that it is reluctant to change. This resistance is the expression of the body's innate wisdom, and most often the body induces it due to a lack of tissue integrity, e.g. the tissue is not strong enough to rise to the occasion. On a more subtle level, people often cling to old ideas, past griefs, resentments that block the acceptance of a higher vitality. [See the book, *Passion Play*, for more information on the Native American Mirror Technique and how to overcome emotional and mental states that cause ill health at www.apple-a-daypress.com.]

The body needs time to re-build the tissue's integrity so it can rise to a more optimal homeostatic level. The obstacle is that often the tissue has lost its inherent blueprint (RNA/DNA telomere information), so the homeostasis mechanism must react against the therapeutic agents. This diminishment of the therapy's impact happens before it can effect a cure. At this point, new symptoms can arise which are side effects of the therapy and cause further discouragement.

The Chinese Dance with Homeostasis. In Chinese herbology, it is common practice to change the herbal, medicinal formula every 10-12 days. This is because 10-12 days is the amount of time it generally takes for homeostasis to effect a significant modification of the herbal therapy. If the patient doesn't realize a cure in this amount of time, the herbalist will change the formula to introduce a new healing influence so the body's homeostasis principle will not be specifically maintained against the therapy. This technique introduces new directions in supporting the health—a "beating around the bush" positive approach to support the healing process from different directions.

"So what traditional herbalists are dealing with here is a law of diminishing return in the therapy timeline. The longer a beneficial therapy is applied, the less effective it becomes because the body's homeostasis modifies any influence that significantly alters the status quotient."

—*A.S. Wheelwright, Lecture, Dallas, Texas 1987*

Bio-Function Formulas Cooperate. With the Bio-Function formulas, Wheelwright combined herbs according to their bio-energetic compatibility, their polarization compatibility, and their ability to be synergistic (allow self-enhancing electron shells to form in the bio-energetic matrix). The result was that he was able to use powerful, therapeutic herbs in an unprecedented safe, gentle, and effective way. The individual herbs not only enhanced each other, they buffered each other's abrasive properties that could cause un-useful side effects. This allows the formula to accomplish its healing work with less unnecessary activity. Wheelwright was an avid admirer of the Law of Economy and sought the direct healing route in his research.

With this approach, he brought herbology out of its historic "allopathic" approach to healing as evidenced by the practice of giving 'cooling' herbs if the patient has a fever, or giving 'heating' herbs such as cayenne if the patient has cold hands and feet; and introduced a more gentle 'neutral' force that would work smoothly and not alert homeostasis to effect the law of diminishing returns as readily. Thus, his Bio-Function formulas gained a reputation as being "the ones that work" amongst health professionals because they cooperated more efffectively with the Laws of Natural Healing. Even so, there still remained an element of homeostatic resistance to the Bio-Function formulas as well—and that he addressed with the Bio-Commands.

The Bio-Command Tool. The Bio-Command formulas change the focus of the Bio-Function formula's intent without disturbing the fundamental balance. They allow the Bio-Function formula to exert its essential support of the targeted tissue in all tissue endeavors, but they bring a special enhancement to a specific tissue activity and thus change the tone of the formula. To clarify, the formula R (Lung) supports the lungs in all its inherent activities including: activation (3 a.m. to 5 a.m.), building, healing, anti-bacterial, anti-fungal and anti-abnormal cell processes. To capitalize on the lung's anti-bacterial activities, the R (Lung) formula can be "commanded" with the #3 (Bactrex) formula to enhance that endeavor. When the #3 is added, there is a new therapeutic direction, which to some extent, re-sets the homeostatic clock on the law of diminishing returns and gives new life to the therapy.

"With the Bio-Commands, we are able to consistently nourish the targeted tissue and cooperate with the body's innate healing processes via the balanced influences of the Bio-Function formula, yet change the therapy's focus enough [change Bio-Command formulas] to maintain an active healing initiative without the healing process being significantly modified by homeostasis. In other words, my formulas apply a neutral, nour-

ishing, healing force that does not quickly play into homeostasis. It does not threaten the Vital Force with too much of a good thing or cause too many overly aggressive changes that might be perceived by the body as being too aggressive. Healing must be gentle and cooperative with the body's directives to be genuinely effective."

—A.S. Wheelwright, 1988

Instead of only a few days of effectiveness with an herb, now a person can take a formula for the full time it takes to restore the tissue to its optimal function—a process that often takes 40 to 160 days depending on the many factors governing natural healing including detoxification, collagen integrity, re-patterning of individual cells, rebuilding of tissue function (groups of organized cells), and bio-energetic (meridian) balance, plus the cooperation of related body systems.

A simple summary of Wheelwright's research and the homeostasis principle is that he figured out a way to administer powerful herbal therapies without alarming the body's homeostatic regulatory function. This phase of his research resulted in the Bio-Function formulas that gently build the integrity of the tissue so the tissue can function at a higher level. Further, one aspect of the Bio-Command formulas is that they significantly change the action of the Bio-Function formula without altering its innate drive to heal and balance the targeted tissue system. This means that the homeostatic law of diminishing returns is avoided and the therapy continues at a more optimal pace.

Challenge #2: Unwanted Side Effects

In herbology, the healing influence of herbs is often based on the body's reaction against the herbs meaning that the herbs have side effects. Thus, there are two kinds of side effects: 1) those that result in activating the beneficial healing/restorative process which causes the body to make changes; and 2) unwanted side effects where the herbal therapy, while helping with one tissue's healing, indirectly injures another tissue or causes new symptoms to manifest. [More in *The Healing Triad: Your Liver—Your Lifeline* (Tips) at www.apple-a-daypress.com.]

Aside Comment: It is due to ignorance of the innate healing faculties of herbs amongst both herbalists and governmental regulatory agencies that have resulted in the loss of several wonderful herbs from the marketplace as they become "not generally recognized as safe" when people misuse them or uninformed researchers overdose rats or elicit damage from isolated ingredients. Many of the herbs currently labeled "unsafe" are indeed wonderful, healing herbs in the hands of competent herbalists. And like all therapeutic agents, their misuse can result in detrimental effects. Because herbs cannot be patented, there are those who lobby to discredit the healing power of herbs and tout specious dangers to cause fear in the public consciousness.

Wheelwright was a master of combinetic herbology—what mixes with what to minimize side effects and maximize the benefits. Thus he was able to design very potent formulas that are both safe and effective.

Prudence & Judgement: Sometimes the repeated use of an herb causes side effects that can elicit the very symptoms for which the herb was recommended. This is called a "proving" whereby overuse of an herb causes the symptoms—often the very symptoms it was intended to cure. For example, the herb Golden Seal (*Hydrastis canadensis*) is often recommended for sinus infections, yet its overuse (in a patient whose health is restored) can cause the nose to run with a thick, stringy, yellow discharge—just like a sinus infection. Further, biochemists point out that prolonged use of high amounts of golden seal can deplete B-vitamins and can also disrupt glucose metabolism. This does not mean that Golden Seal is a dangerous herb. It just needs to be used in the right amount with the right buffering herbs, and for the right amount of time; or as Wheelwright often said, "with prudence and judgment." When Wheelwright used Golden Seal in a formula, he often included additional B-Vitamins in the formula matrix as a natural enhancing ingredient. His 'team approach' to herbology resulted in formulations that capitalize on the herbs inherent healing qualities and minimize side effects.

The Bio-Command Solution to Unwanted Side-Effects

Wheelwright intended that the Bio-Command formulas provide a method for the herbalist or natural health practitioner to keep the healing impetus of the Bio-Function formula active for extended periods of time without having side effects of the therapeutic activity. This has become an issue of primary importance because today, more than ever before, people have chronic degeneration of tissue and require longer periods of time to effect full restoration of tissue integrity and tissue function.

Further, people have an accumulation of zenobiotic agents in their systems including heavy metals, chemicals, radiation, preservatives, and food additives. These toxins interfere with the tissue's ability to function and their removal and drainage must be considered before the tissue can recover its integrity.

While traveling, teaching, and learning in China in the late 1940's, Wheelwright discovered that the Chinese herbal tradition historically had been applied to people who could recover their health in relatively short periods of time. Even the constitutional therapeutics could affect a curative balance within a few days to a few weeks.

"However, today, due to a host of new influences that weaken the body in profound ways such as the empty harvest of modern agriculture; the addition of pesticides, hormones and preservatives to the food supply; the introduction of toxic vaccinations; the retention of mutated bacteria due to the use of antibiotics; the prevalence of mercury in dental fillings and jaw cavitations from root canals; the presence of nuclear radiation in our atmosphere; the petrochemically polluted air; and exposure to disruptive electromagnetic fields; (to name a few); it takes longer for the body to achieve its full genetic potential of tissue integrity and function. Now we must have herbal therapies that can be used for extended periods of time without inflicting negative side effects."

—*A.S. Wheelwright, Austin, Texas 1986*

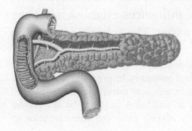

The Pancreas As An Example. What Wheelwright was referring to can be exemplified in the work of restoring the pancreas and it's proper insulin/glucagon regulation of blood sugar metabolism and the domino effects of its imbalance as evidenced by

51

the Syndrome X symptoms of elevated blood pressure, obesity, cancer, polycystic ovaries, strokes, elevated cholesterol, athro- and arterio- sclerosis, etc. [See: *The Weight Is Over* (Tips) for more information about nutrition, diet, and Syndrome X at www.apple-a-daypress.com.]

Today, as opposed to a hundred years ago, we find that the pancreas is pandemically enlarged due to the constant onslaught of post-industrial revolution processing and refinement of starch/sugar foods: wheat, rice, corn, cane, beets, and potatoes. Thus, by the time a 30 year-old person seeks herbal cure of hypoglycemic symptoms, the pancreas has been abused for 29.5 years, secreted the insulin that formerly would have taken 200 years to accomplish, and may have other, inherited weaknesses from the parents.

The body does not achieve a cure to this condition in a few days because the tissue itself is altered. Instead, the body must work with the laws of natural cure and rebuild the pancreas and related organ systems over a reasonable amount of time—the time it takes for the cells to live, reproduce, regenerate, and die in significant numbers to effect a new tissue integrity provided the cellular identity matrix is available to the process. Wheelwright proffered that this could be done in 4.5 months provided that the person adhere to the tenets of the Pro-Vita! dietary pattern [see *The Pro-Vita! Plan for Optimal Nutrition* (Tips) at www.apple-a-daypress.com], and take the Bio-Function formulas P (Pancreas) and Ps (Pancreas-S) along with a rotation of Bio-Commands #2 (Builder), 5 (Stabilizer), #1 (Activator) and # 6 Healer).

Note: Wheelwright also had a concern regarding viral and retro-viral damage to the pancreas from vaccines such as the oral polio vaccine. Regarding this iatrogenic[6] damage, he designed the formula ATAK (Immune Rejuvenator) to help the body get rid of intranoidal, mutated, and acquired disease-causing pathogens.

When the Bio-Command formula is added to the Bio-Function formula, both the bio-energy and the biochemical influences establish a healing stimulus with the body and the targeted tissue. The subsequent rotation

---

[6] Iatrogenic — Induced inadvertently by the medical treatment or procedures or activity of a physician. Applied to any adverse condition in a patient occurring as the result of treatment by a physician or surgeon, especially to infections acquired by the patient during the course of treatment, or complications arising from the administration of drugs.

of the Bio-Command formula (often at two-week intervals) changes both the bio-energetic and biochemical influence of the continued therapy; and thus establishes a new relationship with the body's homeostatic mechanism—one that allows smooth, gentle, thorough healing without pushing the homeostatic watchdog to act against the healing effort.

By this method, a person can benefit from the tissue-supportive influences of the appropriate and needed formula for an extended time—the duration that the body needs to establish new cells, new tissue integrity, optimal tissue function, and thus claim the nutrients and effect cure.

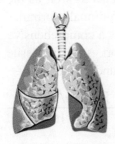 Here's an example of how Bio-Command formulas can accomplish an unprecedented effectiveness in clinical practice. For this example, let's take the case of a person who's smoked cigarettes for 20 years and now has stopped. We all know that stopping smoking is a tremendous accomplishment and a huge step toward better health. But we also know that people who used to smoke are still much more susceptible to cancer later in life. So here, we want to design an herbal program to help the body overcome the effects of smoking and re-establish a new tissue integrity in the lungs. This program would also be applicable for those who have a susceptibility to bronchitis or pneumonia. This process will involve the cleansing, rebuilding, and renewal (regeneration) of the lungs' cells including the re-establishing of the DNA matrix (cellular identity) that has been damaged by the effects of smoking. Here is one such strategy:

Lung Tissue Toning Wellness Program

For people who:

1. Stopped smoking (still have a significantly higher incidence of lung cancer.)
2. Have had bronchitis (exhibits inherent weakness and susceptibility).
3. Have had pneumonia (Wheelwright believed that the use of antibiotics can establish intranoidal residue of dormant, mutated bacteria in the extra-cellular matrix and pleural cavity).

4. Have parental history of emphysema or tuberculosis (miasm[7]).

5. Experience now or have a history of asthma (altered immunity).

6. Live or work in an air-polluted environment (environment needs to be improved to improve the lung's hygiene) such as hair salons, photography labs, dry cleaners, bars, etc.

Strategy. You will notice in the forthcoming example that the one constant is the Bio-Function R (Lung) formula—the one Wheelwright designed to support the lung matrix bio-energetically as well as biochemically via the herbal components. To that "hub" formula is added a changing sequence of Bio-Command formulas as well as the application of the Dragon Rising (Chinese Constitutional) formulas based on the Chinese 5-Element Theory. Thus, this is a comprehensive protocol that weaves together constitutional support, specific tissue support, and varying directives from the Bio-Command formulas.

Bio Function	+ Bio Command	+ Dragon Rising	Frequency/ Duration
1 cap R (Lung)	+ 1 cap #5 (Stabilizer)	+ 1 Metal Sedate	*tid,* for 10 days
Then			
2 caps R (Lung)	+ 2 caps #3 (Bactrex)	+ 2 Metal Sedate	bid, for 10 days
Then			
2 caps R (Lung)	+ 2 caps #4 (FungDx)	+ 2 Metal Sedate	*bid*, for 10 days
Then			
1 cap R (Lung)	+ 1 cap #1 (Activator)	+ 1 Metal Tonify	*tid*, for 10 days
Then			
1 cap R (Lung)	+ 1 cap #2 (Builder)	+ 1 Metal Tonify	*tid*, for 10 days
Then			
2 caps R (Lung)	+ 1 cap #6 (Restore)	+ 2 Metal Tonify	*tid*, for 10 days

---

[7] Miasm — a constitutional predisposition to a specific disease.

Supplies Required For 60-day Protocol:

- R (Lung) .... 240 caps ....4 bottles
- #1 (Activator)..... 30 caps ....1 bottle
- #2 (Builder) ...... 30 caps ....1 bottle
- #3 (Bactrex)...... 60 caps ....1 bottle
- #4 (FungDx)...... 60 caps ....1 bottle
- #5 (Stabilizer)..... 30 caps ....1 bottle
- #6 (Restore) ...... 30 caps ....1 bottle
- Metal Sedate..... 110 caps ....2 bottles
- Metal Tonify..... 120 caps ....2 bottles

Complimentary Formulas:
(Can be added for further comprehensive support if needed by the individual case.)

- Hcv (Heart Cardiovascular) - supports circulation (Pulmonary System).
- SENG (Lymphagest) - supports circulation of the lymph and pleura.

Healing Without Side Effects. Wheelwright was a master of herbal combining so that the body could benefit from the healing power of herbs and be spared the aggravating side effects. Like Dr. Samuel Hahnemann, the founder of homeopathy, who spent the latter years of his life developing the LM water potencies to minimize the healing aggravations and suffering often elicited by the body's reaction to high-potency remedies, Wheelwright spent the last years of his life devising a system of healing that would minimize side effects and suffering at the hands of therapeutic herbology and naturopathic cleansing treatments.

Challenge #3: Diffusion, Dissipation of Herbal Therapies Throughout the Body

As with any nutritional therapy, herbal therapy is ingested and distributed throughout the body. From there, the body, in its inherent intelligence, has the ability to deliver the nutrition to the area needing its ministrations via the bloodstream. However, this natural process does have attrition resulting in diminished results; thus there are different degrees of efficiency. This accounts for one reason why one person gets great results with only a few doses and another gets only mild relief after many doses. Wheelwright wanted a solution that brought more success to more people.

For example: a person takes 1000 mg of vitamin C plus 10 grams of gelatin with the goal to rebuild the extra-cellular matrix (collagen) of the kidneys. The body absorbs 400 mg of the vitamin C and the rest is bound up in the intestines to be excreted in the stool. Of the 400 mg absorbed, 200 mg. gets waylaid as a metabolite for detoxification by the liver; 50 mg is used by the immune system to control bacteria. And so 150 mg gets involved with the kidney repair. A similar story occurs with the gelatin which has attrition in the intestines and is used in other body processes with only a portion being available to rebuild the protein matrix of the kidneys. Thus it is common that there is significant attrition in delivering the healing nutrients to the targeted tissue.

Wheelwright researched the impact of nutrients and herbs on the body tissues. He was particularly intrigued with the research of Dr. Royal Lee and the use of cellular identity factors. Wheelwright worked with Dr. Lee and often proclaimed that Lee was the greatest nutritional genius of the 20th Century. Wheelwright related how Dr. Lee encouraged him to advance herbology to new frontiers as he (Dr. Lee) was doing with nutrition. Wheelwright felt commissioned by Lee to specialize in herbal nutrition whereas Lee's research remained in food-based, therapeutic nutrition.

Cellular Identity Factors

One of Dr. Lee's many breakthroughs[8] was in the application of "cellular identity factors" which he described as the innate function of enzyme-determinants on protein synthesis. Cellular identity factors are the infinitely variable and unique catalysts that construct the matrices upon which cells organize their structure and function. They are unique to each tissue and to each part of each tissue. Thus the cells of every tissue have multiplicities of enzymes and nucleo-proteins that form the blueprint for the tissue's structure and activity. As archetypal blueprints, these identity factors are necessary for the construction and repair of the tissue and determine the effectiveness of its function. In the bio-energetic or quantum physics perspective, the cellular identity matrix resonates to the innate vitality pattern of the tissue, and is the core structure upon which the tissue is organized.

---

[8] Lee capitalized on the work of forerunners: Drs. George Crile, T. B. Robertson, and F.B. Turck who discovered aspects of how cells grow and repair themselves from their unique, "life-given" blueprints.

Wheelwright incorporated cellular identity factors into his herbal research because the cellular identity factors are the blueprints of healthy tissue structure and function. When there is degeneration of a tissue, it cannot function properly. When the cellular identity is lost, the tissue no longer has the blueprint to rebuild its integrity, despite the cleansing, building, of the tissue as well as the resulting improvement in circulation. Wheelwright saw cellular identity as a missing component in nutritional healing because the general trend in human nutrition over the past hundred years had drifted away from sources of these types of nutrients so that the raw materials were no longer abundant for the body's use in maintaining tissue integrity.

Beyond providing vitamins, minerals, enzymes, amino acids and other nutrients for the body to use, the cellular identity factors are food-elements that support the very integrity of a tissue. They are the first organic structures that arise with a determinant or intelligence as opposed to inorganic compounds that do not express life. Many instances of people's symptoms are based on tissue weakness or an organ that is not functioning properly. Often, the tissue has lost its cellular identity and it is not producing new cells of high integrity. Thus it can only function in a state of weakness and it is lacking the inherent blueprint to repair itself properly. Its cells are producing a poor quality of collagen, lacking structure, and exhibiting weakened function. The basic blueprint, the nucleo-proteins and enzymators, can be supplied nutritionally.

When a tissue is weak and unable to renew it's innate integrity, supplements such as vitamins, minerals, enzymes, and other nutritional factors including herbal nutrition can fail to fully help the ailing tissue because fundamentally the tissue is lacking its innate blueprint to guide the healing and rejuvenation efforts. Wheelwright called this "building your house on sand" meaning that if the foundation is weak, all the steel and high quality components used in the construction fail to build a truly strong structure.

How does tissue lose its cellular identity? This degeneration occurs with the aging process as the telomeres (sometimes called "junk DNA"—the natural end of a eukaryotic chromosome) are depleted from the ends of the tissue's inherent DNA strands during cellular mitosis (reproduction). This occurs during normal cellular reproduction and is accelerated by free-radical damage, x-radiation, and other cell-damaging phenomenon including viral, bacterial, fungal, and parasitic presence. The cancer process can more easily alter tissues that have a weak cellular identity.

Telomeres are the physical ends of linear eukaryotic chromosomes. They are specialized nucleoprotein complexes that have important functions, primarily in the protection, replication, and stabilization of the chromosome ends. In most organisms studied, telomeres contain lengthy stretches of tandemly repeated simple DNA sequences composed of a G-rich strand and a C-rich strand (called terminal repeats). These terminal repeats are highly conserved; in fact all vertebrates appear to have the same simple sequence repeat in telomeres: (TTAGGG)n. Often sequences adjacent to the telomeric repeats are highly polymorphic, are rich in DNA repetitive elements (termed subtelomeric repeats), and in some cases, genes have been found in the proterminal regions of chromosomes.

[TelDB Copyright Washington University School of Medicine.]

The process of losing cellular identity is similar to making a photocopy of a photocopy, of a photocopy, of a photocopy. Once this is done a few times, the resulting document has lost its crispness and picked up a few aberrations. If, in cellular mitosis, the new cell is not as crisp as the parent cell, it loses some of its identity. Thus, it cannot function as well. Further, as the extra-cellular matrix loses its identity and thus becomes weak, the tissue itself loses integrity and becomes weak. This is the genetic process of aging. Wheelwright was at the forefront of the anti-aging research from a basic nutritional viewpoint long before it came into vogue in the 1990's.

Wheelwright surmised that, while herbs could help an ailing or weakened tissue perform better, the true restoration of health involved helping the cells re-discover their identity and manifest a stronger vitality, regain tissue integrity, and perform their function more effectively. The key to restoration of tissue health is based on the cell's ability to re-build itself and function better. With the cellular identity 'food' factors, denoted RNA/DNA factors, Wheelwright found a nutritional component that worked at the very core of healing by supplying the specific enzymes and fundamentally unique nucleo-proteins that the tissue requires for healing.

Cellular identity factors are the alphabet of the cellular intelligence. They remind the tissues how to construct and re-construct their fundamental structures so that they function properly. This key nutritional component is lacking in most of today's vitamin, mineral, protein, and herbal supplements. It is vitally important in the healing of weakened, damaged, aged, tissues; and without it, the tissue can never fully recover its optimal function.

—A.S. Wheelwright, discussion with nutritionists, Austin, Texas 1986

 Wheelwright was also particularly fond of the general, broad-spectrum cellular identity factors from the very basic cellular structure of a type of nutritional yeast organism, *Saccharomyces cerevisiae*. In his research, he found that the basic sequences and their components were somewhat universal and that the human body could use them as "generic tools" to help reconstruct its tissue integrity to some extent. They are not as specifically applicable as the RNA/DNA food factors, but instead provide life-organized identity factors for general use anywhere in the body. Here we find a fundamental link between human beings and simple cellular structures. This link exists between plants, animals, and humans as the basic blueprints of certain cellular activities are derived from similar patterns.

Basic, general cellular identity factors. *Recent work has yielded considerable information concerning the structure and function of telomeres and their associated sequences in the budding yeast Saccharomyces cerevisiae. The structure and maintenance of* *telomeres depends not only on the RNA template and the catalytic subunit of telomerase, but on a number of other proteins. These include proteins involved in assessing DNA damage and cell cycle regulation. There are also non-telomerase mediated processes involved in the normal maintenance of telomeres. In addition to proteins involved in telomere maintenance, there are a number of other proteins involved in the chromatin structure of the region. Many of these proteins have roles in silencing, aging, segregation and nuclear architecture. The structure of the subtelomeric regions has been well characterized and consists of a mosaic of repeats found in variable copy numbers and locations. Amidst the variable mosaic elements there are small conserved sequences found at all ends that may have functional roles. Recent work shows that the subtelomeric repeats can rescue chromosome ends when telomerase fails, buffer subtelomerically located genes against transcriptional silencing, and protect the genome from deleterious rearrangements due to ectopic recombination. Thus the telomeres of yeast have a variety of roles in the life of the yeast cell beyond the protection of the ends and overcoming the end replication problem associated with linear molecules.*

Institute of Molecular Medicine, John Radcliffe Hospital, Oxford OX3 9DS, United Kingdom; fax: +44-(0) 1865-222-500

Copyright (C) 2003 BioProt Network

In addition to the biology and biochemistry of nutrition, Wheelwright applied the quantum physics of bio-energy and found that the cellular identity factors greatly enhanced the overall bio-energetic matrix of an herbal/nutritional formula. Since they are structures organized by the very process of Life Itself, they form in concord with the innate resonance pattern of a tissue.

By including cellular identity factors with a more judicious selection of herbs and constructing the formulation so that its bio-energetic resonance is tuned to the optimal tissue frequency, Wheelwright launched a new dimension in herbal nutrition and natural healing.

60

"Except for air, water, sunshine, and ch'i-energy; all nutrition is based on the life signatures of plants—be it the minerals, vitamins, proteins, saccharides, lipids, and enzymes in the plant; or the plant matrix incorporated into the animal-kingdom products humanity uses for food. The only rational, logical extension of how a human being exists in Nature is that the plants serve as medicines and have the power to restore physical health. Even more, the subtle energy of plants can impact the emotional and mental regions with their essences."

—*A.S. Wheelwright, conversation with Jack Tips, 1988*

Orchestra analogy. For an analogy that emphasizes the role of the Bio-Command formulas, consider a symphony orchestra. In an orchestra there are many different instruments that can all play the note, A-440. However, the tonal qualities of the trumpet are quite different than the bassoon, even though the resonance of the note is 440 vibratory cycles per second. Each instrument's tone creates different responses in the human psyche. The trumpet can give a clarion blast and a call to action where as the bassoon can create a mellow, melancholy flow. Thus we find that martial music capitalizes on the characteristics of the stimulating brass instruments and does not often attempt to use an oboe and a tympani to rouse people to patriotic fervor. Reciprocally, a haunting, solitary flute and a meditative violin, while playing the same note-alphabet as a Sousa martial march, can lead a person to a peaceful, reflective state of mind.

In the Wheelwright Healing System, the Bio-Function formula is the "note"—the resonance pattern and tissue nutrition—and the Bio-Command formula is the instrument lending a tonal quality that can lead the music to a specific enhancement. The Bio-Function formula can hone in on the tissue because it has the resonance pattern and cellular identity factors. The Bio-Command specifies particular enthusiasm for a specific endeavor.

The Swiss physician and researcher, Dr. Paul Niehans[9], found that the body's innate intelligence would send the necessary nutrients and tissue factors to the appropriate tissue. His work with embryonic cells showed that if a person were injected with embryonic thyroid cells, those cells would migrate or hone in on the thyroid and work with that specific tissue. The injected cells bear the cellular identity and resonance pattern of thyroid. The body, in its innate wisdom, delivers those structures to the thyroid for rejuvenation. Niehans' research showed that the body could recognize molecular structures and deliver them to where they are most appropriate such as iodine migrating to the thyroid.

Targeted Nutrition. Wheelwright applied the same principles in his herbal nutrition by creating formulas that the body would send to a specific tissue where it would be most effective. In this way, he was able to do more with less. Both the cellular identity factors and the tissue-tuned resonance pattern of Wheelwright's formulas help hone in on the target tissue and deliver an unprecedented level of specific nutrition to the targeted tissue.

Often the loosely held Doctrine Of Signatures provides a glimpse of the universality of form and function. Cauliflower looks like the brain and in it are food factors that specifically support the brain. Pimiento peppers are heart-shaped and provide factors to support the heart. The sea sponge resembles thyroid tissue and it has influence on that gland via its iodine. Herbs often have some physical characteristic that suggests the part of the body they have an affinity for. Without taking it to extreme; or dwelling on the numerous exceptions; or mentioning bananas, coco-de-mer, etc.; the point here simply leads us to consider

---

[9] Paul Niehans is a Swiss doctor who gained fame for inventing and then developing cellular therapy, a method he has successfully applied to thousands of patients. In 1955, he treated Pope Pious XII and, as a token of gratitude, he was nominated a member of the Vatican Academy of Science, following in the foot-steps of Sir Alexander Flemming, the father of penicillin. He has also treated many crowned heads, presidents, celebrities and film stars.

affinities and correlations of the countless "variations on a theme" of life's organization patterns.

With most nutritional formulas, as is certainly the case with vitamins and minerals, the nutritive molecules are distributed throughout the body. The entire amount is not delivered to a specific tissue. With Wheelwright's formulas, he found a way to deliver more of the benefits to the specific tissue. With the addition of the Bio-Command formula, Wheelwright was able to design programs with an unheard of precision—specific to a targeted tissue with an enhanced directive to a specific benefit.

Challenge #4: Dosage Effectiveness (The Law of Mass Action and Tissue Response)

Wheelwright's research with targeted nutrition directly impacts the biochemical processes of healing. In nutritional biochemistry, the *Law of Mass Action*[10] plays the same role as it does in drug medicine. Simply put, it takes a certain amount of a substance to effectively impact a body response on the biochemical level—the more catalysts, the bigger the reaction.

For example, 1-mcg. of the thyroid drug medication, Synthroid®, is not enough to temporarily normalize a person's hypothyroid condition by providing enough thyroxin activity to cause the body to function properly; but 25-mcg. to 300-mcg. is enough to facilitate the necessary thyroxin activity for metabolic balance. In another example, 1-mcg of Vitamin C is not enough to cure scurvy, but 2000-mg every four hours will effect a cure.

The Law of Mass action is applicable to the molecular, biochemical aspect of a human being; but in quantum physics there are different laws that are also operative. One is the Law of Resonance where a vibratory pattern can affect countless other vibratory patterns via a wave form. Another is the theory that an electron can be in more than one place at a time.

---

[10] Law of Mass Action - an empirical law stating that the rate of a chemical reaction is proportional to the molecular concentrations of the reacting substances. (e.g. the more dynamite, the bigger the explosion.)

The Quest For The Lower Dose To Bring Greater Effectiveness

An important issue in nutrition is the proper dosage because the body needs enough 'mass action' to effect proper results, yet a dose that is too big can cause other imbalances. Both "too little" and "too much" are problematic. In his early research, Wheelwright was concerned with the high dosages of food-based supplementation needed to obtain the proper effects. He approached his mentor, Dr. Royal Lee and confronted this issue. At the time, Lee was manufacturing wonderful nutritional formulas, but people often had to take 30 or 40 tablets a day for long periods of time to get enough "mass action" to realize curative leverage.

Not only was taking massive amounts of manufactured supplements inconvenient to the patients, foul-tasting (as the preferred method of administration was chewing the tablets), and time consuming (due to the length of the programs); it was expensive to buy bottle after bottle of a manufactured supplement. All of these factors worked against patient compliance in the real world of day-to-day life.

One of the reasons so many tablets were required was that without concentrated nutrients (such as manufactured vitamins and concentrated minerals which many researchers consider 'unnatural',) the natural food products are low in therapeutic catalysts. This is because foods are generally in the "pot-herb" and occasionally in the "tonic" categories; thus they are provided by Nature for daily on-going use and are not strongly therapeutic in their action. For example, we find that brewer's yeast contains Vitamin B-12, but it would take a huge bucket full to get the therapeutic action of the synthetic, supplemental form. This fact caused even the great natural-source proponent, Dr. Royal Lee, to include synthetic vitamins in some of his food-based formulas.

Wheelwright found the solution in combinetic herbology:

"Food can be your medicine, but you've got to have a lot of patience. Herbal therapies work much quicker as they are the 'foods' for healing."

—A.S. Wheelwright in an address to practitioners, 1989

Wheelwright suggested using herbs to provide more powerful nutrients (enzymes, proteins, vitamin co-factors, minerals, saccharides, etc.) along with food factors because herbs were natural foods that provided therapeutic actions. Lee declined to pursue herbs in his research, already having more research to accomplish than one lifetime would permit, but with Lee's encouragement, Wheelwright independently advanced the herbal research that years later would come to fruition as the Systemic formulations.

Law of Economy. Wheelwright believed in the Law of Economy (doing the most with the least) and knew instinctively that the restoration of tissue integrity and health could come without having to laboriously take numerous tablets. (Molecular biology vs. quantum physics.) It was an additional benefit of the 'targeting' effect (the compatible bio-energetic resonance pattern plus cellular identity factors) that solved the dissipation of nutrients throughout the body, combined with the directive of the Bio-Command formulas and their ability to increase the effectiveness of the program, that brought forth an herbal healing system whereby true healing results could be obtained with much smaller dosages. Instead of 30 to 40 tablets daily providing the proper "mass action;" in Wheelwright's healing system, only 2 to 4 capsules daily were required. This solved the issue of patient compliance from the convenience, taste and cost perspective.

Natural vs. Synthetic. Wheelwright researched the vitamins, particularly the B complex vitamins, and found herbal enzymators for each vitamin. He found that even U.S. Pharmacopoeia (USP) vitamins could be introduced into a plant matrix, share electrons, and gain a "living" warp; and thus be more suitable for human nutritional therapy. Although Wheelwright was an avid proponent of food-based, natural vitamins, he found that small amounts of USP vitamins could be combined with specific herbs and a natural base of plant-source vitamins such as yeast, and result in a strong therapeutic action willingly accepted by the body. He corroborated his findings with the Russian researcher, Semyon Kirlian[11] whose photographs were being used to exemplify the striking difference between a natural vitamin and a synthetic analog.

---

[11] Kiliian's work was originally believed to photographically record the aura of living things, but his research was not reproduced in a vacuum. Thus it is surmised that his photographic technique portrays the corona discharge of life forms as their temperature and bio-energy affects the moisture in the air.

The incorporation of vitamins into the herbal matrix surprised Wheelwright and many of his devotees as it weakened the battle line in the synthetic vs. natural vitamin argument where the naturalists condemned synthetic vitamins despite their success in clinical studies, and the orthomolecular physicians condemned natural supplements as being too weak and non-standardized in their potency. Perhaps now, with hindsight, we see that because of Wheelwright's open mind and dedication to "the facts", he discovered how a living organism is an alchemical factory that can, when necessary, take molecules apart and put them back together so they support life processes. He used to tease the "all natural devotees" who preached "everything organic" with the fact that the human body itself makes an inorganic compound. On the brink of their well-ordered view collapsing, they would demand, "What?" Wheelwright's eyes would twinkle and he'd smile and say, "Hydrochloric acid—something you'd die without." And leave them to ponder the incompleteness of their philosophy, often not realizing that Wheelwright was one of the major proponents of the "life begets life" philosophy. Wheelwright had previously initiated a controversial position on the relationship between synthetic vitamin E and infant mortality that actually started the rapid increase in public awareness about the difference between synthetic and natural supplements.

Wheelwright also studied various forms of Vitamin C—from the common ascorbic acid (then a by-product of the Zanzibar paper industry), to sago palm, calcium ascorbate, rose hips, Indian amla, rare Brazilian plants, camu camu, orange, acerola cherry, lemon, and buffered forms. He found that actually all forms of Vitamin C were mildly toxic to the body, even with their bioflavanoid components intact, and cited that fact as a reason the body quickly used and disposed of it via urinary excretion. He also found that each form of Vitamin C had an affinity to perform a different, necessary role in the body—some to help excrete heavy metals, some to build collagen, some to kill bacteria and even some viral forms, and some necessary to the liver's complex detoxification pathways. Thus he was able to make advancements in the arena of vitamin nutrition.

Wheelwright soon discovered that with the bio-energetically-designed formulas, the duration of the therapeutic programs was greatly reduced as well as the dosages. For example, before Wheelwright, it was considered standard operating procedure for a liver rebuilding program to require two years using diet and food-supplements. Knowing this, people were taking 30 to 40 tablets a day for two years to bring their livers to a more optimal functional level. Wheelwright changed this when he was able to help the body achieve an optimal liver functional level by applying two to four capsules daily of his two liver formulas enhanced by one capsule of a Bio-Command. Thus the herbal therapies could do the job of 40 tablets by applying only 5 capsules. And the duration of the program? Only four months! Wheelwright soon found that people could, in the 'real world', dedicate themselves to doing what was necessary with a simple program for a realistic amount of time. [This is discussed in detail in the book, *The Healing Triad—Your Liver, Your Lifeline* at www.apple-a-daypress.com.]

The smaller doses and shorter duration to achieve healing further supported Wheelwright's opinion that a properly designed formula would solicit the help of the body's innate healing mechanism. He always maintained that no one—no doctor, no nutritionist, no philosopher, no healer—knows better than the body about how to heal itself. He believed that God already installed the healing mechanism in the body. He felt that the role of the practitioner/healer was to cooperate with that divine plan, provide the initital impetus or directive to remind the body how to tap into its innate healing capacity, and get out of the way and let the body heal. He considered it the ultimate validation of his research that the body would cooperate so well with his resonance-based formulations.

Challenge #5: Concerns Regarding Drug Interactions

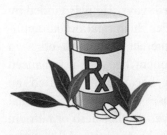

I must preface this topic with the statement that to date, there are no studies to prove or disprove Wheelwright's opinions presented here. However, Wheelwright's opinion, based on his time-proven theories, has been corroborated repeatedly in clinical practice by doctors' observations.

Wheelwright often commented that once his formulas were constructed, a single ingredient did not function quite the same in the body as that ingredient would before it was properly combined in his formula. For example, if a person took 25 mg. of rose hip vitamin C, it would perform a certain way in the body - let's say that 10 mg. would bind with copper, and 15 mg would build collagen. But 25 mg. of rose hips vitamin C combined with other herbs and nutrients in a Wheelwright herbal formula might be totally dedicated to protecting cell membranes because it formed an alliance with the bioflavanoids of the pimiento herb in the formula.

Since the bio-energy changes so dramatically when herbs and nutritive factors are properly combined, Wheelwright also believed that the individual components changed in some fashion as well. He called it *'the biological warp'* of the molecules. Further, the synergistic aspect, in which the combined formula has more bio-energy than the sum total of its parts, proves that something has changed beyond the delivery of random nutrients.

Changes in nutritive factors, depending on their combination with other nutritive factors, are a well-known fact of biochemistry. Free form amino acids must be taken away from milk or they will combine with the proteins in the milk and no longer be available to the body in their free state and thus not have the desired therapeutic effect. Phytates[13] in wheat will bind with zinc and prevent it from being absorbed as a nutrient. The tannins in tea will bind with iron and prevent its absorption. Avadin, an anti-proteolytic agent in raw egg whites, will block the proper absorption of the albumin unless first deactivated by cooking. The list can run into the thousands of biochemical changes that occur when nutrients are combined with other components. The same is true with the nutritive components of herbs.

Combinations, Not Individual Components. Wheelwright was known for combining herbs in unprecedented ways. He was guided by the laws of herbal polarization, bio-energetics, historical herbal applications, and his research of how herbs interact with each other in combinations. He would select one component because it enhanced another. He'd select another component because it nullified an unwanted side effect, and another because it provided additional support to the targeted system. He'd select yet another herb or nutrient because it provided drainage of the metabolic by-products. All this was guided by the resonance pattern and how it would fall into line with the inherent resonance of the tissue's fundamental blueprint.

---

[13] Phytate - A salt or ester of phytic acid which is an inositol hexaphosphate, found in plant cells, especially in seeds, where it acts as a storage compound for phosphate groups.

Hawthorne. So when asked about drug interactions and the herbal formulas, Wheelwright was skeptical of the current position of the U.S. Pharmacopoeia and herbalists who did not understand the principles of his research. He cited that some herbs, such as Hawthorne (*Crategus laevigata, monogyna,* and *oxycantha*), when used in certain small amounts, could slightly enhance the effectiveness of drugs such as digitalis and beta blockers, and thus serve as beneficial components (the herb-drug interaction caused a small improvement). However, large, heroic doses (such doses are never used in his formulations and are generally more than anyone would take) could theoretically contribute to overdosing on the drug. But he felt that the effects of the Hawthorne in his Hcv (Heart-Cardiovascular) formula, because of its association with the formula's Sete Sangrias (herb) and potassium (mineral), could only bring benefit and could never cause a detrimental interaction. And finally, he was quick to cite that the concern regarding negative interactions between Hawthorne and the drugs was only theoretical and that there were no documented case histories of any problem, and certainly not with his formula which he considered further exempt from any likelihood of incompatibility.

He would also cite that with his formulas, because he could do more with less, there was even less chance that there could be unwanted side-effects. In some of the studies that foster concern regarding herb-drug interaction, the amount of the herb must be very high. The concern regarding the use of garlic and the drug Wayfarin™, a person must consume more than 5 grams of raw, fresh garlic; and the concern regarding the herb turmeric (*curcuma longa*) and the use of anti-coagulant medications was based on very high doses of turmeric (more than 15 grams of the dried, powdered herb.)

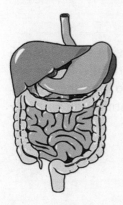 **Cascara segrada.** In another example, the herb, *cascara segrada,* often used as a laxative, was considered to have a potassium-depleting effect for people on diuretics for blood pressure issues, the drug Thiazide™, or steroids. Wheelwright cited that again, his use of *cascara segrada* in his C (Colon) formula was not a concern because he first oxygenated the cascara in the Native American tradition, a process that alters the herb and removes (oxidizes) the 'gripping' effects.

Then, the *cascara segrada* is presented to the body in combination with other herbs that allow it to be more compatible with the colon tissue. Thirdly, his C (Colon) formulation contains potassium as a completing component. As a final point, he cited that his C (Colon) formula did not function as a laxative but as a formula designed to help the body restore colon tissue integrity, hydration, and peristalsis, thus it focuses on the cause of constipation rather than causing an forced expulsion process. The lack of laxative effect in the C (Colon) formula is mystifying to the herbalist who only thinks in terms of known herbal effects. Wheelwright's application of *cascara segrada* as a primary ingredient in tandem with other modifying herbs demonstrates that the herbal combination functions differently than expected in the body and bears testimony to the unique properties of the combinetic formula.

The real issue, according to Wheelwright, was not if a concentrated, extracted, isolated component of an herb could cause side effects. Instead, herb-drug interaction issues should be based on: 1) use of the whole herb and not isolated, concentrated components, 2) the amount used, and 3) what the herb is combined with. This means that herb-drug interactions must be studied in how it's being delivered to the person. More specifically, regarding his formulas, he maintained that the herbs were whole as found in nature, used in smaller amounts because of wise combinations; and that his combinations brought the herbs into further safety because a detrimental effect of the herb would not work in his bio-energetic matrix. This is why he would often claim that his formulas were more powerful and simultaneously gentler than any other formulas. And Wheelwright was quick to provocatively exclaim, "Why would you take a drug? Do you have a deficiency of diethyl-stilbestrol in your diet?"

Challenge #6: Inventory Requirements

From the perspective of practicality, instead of having to inventory a dozen formulas for each tissue and system, practitioners of the Wheelwright Healing System only need one (or two) plus the six Bio-Commands. A conventional herbalist requires 336 formulas in his or her pharmacy to do what 34 Systemic Formulas will do.

In comprehensive programming, inventory does not have to exceed 85 formulas to move freely through the entire Wheelwright Healing System with no limitations. In the Wheelwright Healing System, comprehensive programming means that the following considerations are designed into the program:

1. The terrain that allows the symptom(s)
2. The constitutional state (the struggle of the vital force's circulation of energy)
3. Specific tissue support
4. Specific command enhancement
5. Anti-pathogenic support
6. General nutritional support
7. Drainage support.

Comprehensive Protocol: Hepatitis C. For example, let's design a comprehensive healing program for a person with Hepatitis C concerns and select from the complete Wheelwright offerings:

1. **For the terrain** — select from the two Bio-Basic formulas, in this case: *ACCELL* supports the liver's detoxification processes while simultaneously supporting the immune system and gastrointestinal tract. (The other Bio-Basic formula, ENZEE, could also be used.)

2. **Constitutional state** — select from the 14 Chinese 5-Element formulas: in this case: *General Tonify* supports the liver, spleen, and immune system.

3. **Specific tissue support** — select from the 28 Bio-Function formulas, in this case: *Ls (Liver-s)* and *L (Liver)*. Two of the world's finest liver formulas.

4. **Specific command** — select one of the six Bio-Command formulas, in this case: #5 (Stabilizer) - helps prevent the cirrhosis process and serves in an anti-viral capacity.

5. **Anti-pathogenic** — select from the 19 Bio-Challenge formulas, in this case: *ATAK (Immune Rejuvenator)* - helps correct deep-seated pathogenic infections, and VIVI (Virox) is a specific anti-viral compound.

6. **General Nutrition** — select from the 16 Bio-Nutriments, in this case: *CLR (Chlorophyllium)* to help purify the liver and blood by supporting the nutritional components with trace minerals, vitamins, etc.

7. **Drainage** — select from any category, in this case the ACCELL already provides drainage. Additional support could be gained from the ACX (Vitamin Detox) formula, if needed.

In this categorical approach to comprehensive programming, the most advanced herbal healing system in the world comes down to the simplicity of selecting applicable formulas from seven categories (often with one formula covering more than one category) with an effective program resulting from using several formulas that provide a totally thorough healing dimension - therapeutic healing herbs, nutritional (biochemical) support, and bio-energetic support.

Here's what that basic Hepatitis C program could be:

Before the first meal

1 scoop ACCELL in 6 oz pure water.
2 Ls (Liver-s)
1 CLR (Chlorophyllium)
1 General Tonify
1 #5 (Stabilizer)
1 ATAK (Immune Rejuvenator)

Mid Afternoon

2 L (Liver)
1 CLR (Chlorophyllium)
1 General Tonify
1 ATAK (Immune Rejuvenator)
1 VIVI (Virox)

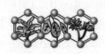

Discourse 3:
The Balance Principle (Allopathy, Homeopathy, and Wheelwright)

The history of herbology is generally an allopathic one meaning that often its philosophical approach is to counter an abnormality with its opposite (*contraria contraris*). In some systems of Chinese herbology, if the spleen is damp, herbs are often given to dry the spleen. If the liver is hot, then herbs are given to cool the liver. In American herbology, if there is a bacterial infection, then herbs are given to kill or interfere with bacteria as well as strengthen the immune response to bacteria. In Aruvedic herbology, if a dosha (constitution state) is weak, then strengthening, counterbalancing herbs are given.

The fact that herbology has allopathic methods is not meant to be a criticism because even when herbs are used allopathically, there is the saving grace of the fact of biological compatibility that is sorely lacking when synthetic drugs are used. The body is able to work with herbs and can more easily balance and counter balance their effects because herbs (tonic and therapeutic herbs) are generally less dictatorial than a chemical drug that demands control of a person's body functions.

Allopathy[14]. There are several inherent problems with an allopathic approach to healing. The first and foremost is that an outside observer (practitioner) does not know or seek to understand the true cause of the problem. The research and resulting therapies seek to alter only the effects or symptoms that are revealed. Thus the allopathic approach is primarily occupied with the treatment of symptoms, not the cause. We see the primitive thought process of western medicine in the nostrums that line the drug store shelves—anti-diarrhea medicines, anti-constipation laxatives, anti-pain analgesics, anti-fever, anti-acids, antibiotics, anti-spasmodics, anti-inflammatories, anti-histamines, anti-itch medi-

---

[14] Allopathy — That system of medical practice which aims to combat disease by the use of remedies which produce effects different from those produced by the special disease treated; a term invented by Hahnemann to designate the ordinary practice, as opposed to homeopathy.

cines, and so forth. They are all anti-symptom preparations but never address the cause.

Symptom-Expression. Since symptoms are the perfect expression of the body's struggle to maintain homeostasis, treatment of symptoms only results in deranging the body's vital expression and leaves the cause of the disturbance to manifest a deeper pathology since its more superficial symptoms (expressions) are suppressed by treatment.

For further clarification, let's consider a fever as a result of an upper respiratory infection. The fever is the body's perfect expression and necessary process for healing the condition. In this example, let's say that an adult has a fever due to an upper respiratory infection. The fever is the body's vital response to restore optimal health. The fever serves many beneficial purposes including the mustering, increase, and mobilization of the immune system's army of bacteria fighters, and it creates a pasteurization process that helps kill the bacteria.

If a person thinks, "Oh no, I have a fever. I have to get rid of the fever!" the resulting anti-febrile medication will inhibit the body's proper and necessary response to the cause of the problem and serves to inhibit the needed immunological processes that would result in the cloning of immune cells for greater future health. "But my fever is making me feel achy and uncomfortable," cries the patient not knowing that the sooner the cause of the fever is corrected, the sooner the fever will depart as a contributor to the victorious restoration of health.

From the naturopathic perspective, the truly valuable thought process is:

Q. What caused the bacteria to proliferate?
A. The terrain was suitable to proliferation.

Q. Why was the terrain suitable to the bacteria? Was it:
   1. A constitutional predisposition (an inherited weakness - genetics, allergy, etc.) that allows on-going infections?

2. An acquired, terrain susceptibility? (i.e. congestion from commercial milk products, exposure to second hand tobacco smoke, xenobiotic toxicity, etc.)

3. Both a constitutional weakness and an acquired terrain ('colds always go to the chest' plus 'been using commercial milk on cereal for past two weeks'.)

4. Strictly due to exposure of a pathogen (bacteria) to which the body had poor immunity (even so, what inhibited the body's ability to respond to it)?

Once the cause is determined, the appropriate therapy can be selected. And the bacteria are seldom the cause. It is an opportunistic infection due to the four terrain questions above. The fever is not the cause. In all cases, inhibiting the body's process to generate a fever has nothing to do with the cause or cure. [The only time to modify the fever would be if the body's reaction was too aggressive, e.g. the fever goes too high in its exuberance.] Thus, the naturopathic treatment will consider and seek to correct the causative factors rather than treating and suppressing the symptoms.

The same process holds true with the cough of this example's upper respiratory infection. The cough is the body's perfect response to rid the lungs of the pathogenic bacteria that has been captured in the mucous secretions. Taking an allopathic "cough suppressant" only hinders the body in getting well. [Yes, as an exception, it may sometimes be necessary to modify the body's cough response when it is too aggressive.] Generally, using an herbal expectorant, rather than a suppressant, would serve the direction of the body's curative processes.

Another problem with an allopathic approach to healing is the side effects of treatment. Western medicine is notorious for dangerous and damaging side effects because most of its medicines are poisonous drugs. (There are generally 150,000 reported deaths a year attributed to drugs and iatrogenic therapies and many more that are unreported as drug-related.) But the allopathically-oriented herbalist can also cause side effects, though rare and certainly a death is a most unlikely occurrence. Mild side effects can occur when too much of a therapeutic herb is used and the body's homeostatic principle must react against the therapy and manifest sideshow symptoms. Today, this is often seen by overuse of therapeutic herbs where people develop symptoms associated with the known "provings" (side effects) of the herb as outlined in the desk references of classical homeopathy known as "Materia Medicas."

Homeopathy[12]. On the other side of the coin from an allopathic approach to healing is a homeopathic approach. Here the guiding philosophy is *similia similibus curentur*, or *let likes be cured by likes*. In homeopathy, the symptoms are understood in their totality (mentally, emotionally, and physically) and a medicine given in a potentized micro-dose based on the fact that a strong and sustained, gross dose would cause a very similar symptom-pattern in a healthy individual.

In the person manifesting a symptom, the homeopathic medicine stimulates the innate vitality to heal everything resembling the gross effects of medicine given. Thus the body heals the cause of the symptoms and accomplishes the restoration of health itself according to its wisdom. Homeopathy has several major and wonderful advantages over allopathic treatment in that it stimulates the body to correct the cause of the problem and restore health according to the principles of natural law. It heals without side-effects, as the infinitesimal doses do not and cannot poison the body; in fact, the side-effect of the medicine is the healing.

Homeopathy, like every healing modality, has limitations when the whole spectrum of a human being is considered. One limitation is that symptoms are required before a proper remedy can be selected. This means that when a person is basically healthy and not manifesting symptoms (mentally, emotionally, physically), there is no basis for advancing health to more optimal dimensions. Homeopathy helps the body back to its best adaptability under the circumstances of identified symptom-states, and helps heal many causes of symptoms; but it usually does not help build tissues for future abundant health beyond what is necessary to function well. This is a particularly important concern for the elderly who have lost tissue integrity and do not have the cellular identity to re-establish healthier tissue. Homeopathy brings

---

[12] Homeopathy — The art of curing, founded on resemblances; the theory and its practice that disease is cured by remedies which produce on a healthy person effects similar to the symptoms of the complaint under which the patient suffers, the remedies being administered in extremely minute (infinitesimal) doses. This system was founded by Dr. Samuel Hahnemann, and is opposed to allopathy.

the body back to its best-possible status quotient, but leaves off at the threshold of on-going preventative health maintenance once the remedy (selected on a symptom/remedy picture) has exerted its influence. At this juncture in homeopathic medicine, it's a "wait and see" position as the prescriber waits to see what symptoms, if any, will develop. Thus the new era of classical homeopaths are finding the need to understand basic nutrition and detoxification so the body can exist in its most advantageous environment and have the basic components required by the vital force to adapt to the impetus of the prescribed remedy.

So, is there a way to build and maintain health when there are no guiding symptoms to point the way? Of course there is. Hahnemann, the founder of homeopathy, established the ability of medicine to treat the individual's core adaptive process—the cause of disease—and restore health. "*The sole mission of the physician is to cure rapidly, gently, permanently.*" Organon of Medicine, 1883. Thus homeopathy excels when there is a clear symptom picture. But Wheelwright was interested in building and improving health, not only when there were symptoms, but on a day to day basis even when a person was asymptomatic. Wheelwright believed that health was a function of daily nutrition, exercise, rest and support of the weakest links. He built his herbal formulas within the neutral range of nourishment so they could build and bolster the various tissues. He taught a dietary philosophy to support the body both biochemically and bio-energetically. [See *The Pro-Vita Plan for Optimal Nutrition* at www.apple-a-daypress.com].

Hahnemann received some of his insights on healing from Paracelsus[13], the ancient alchemist, and developed them from the perspective of drug pathogenesis. But Paracelsus also practiced tincture-herbology for the maintenance and improvement of health along with the rudiments of homeopathic treatment. Hahnemann did not explore this area of work beyond basic hygienic dietary recommendations to correct the patient's foundational terrain e.g. if you are starving to death, don't take a remedy for increased appetite, eat some food.

---

[13] Paracelsus - A Bohemian healer and philosopher who lived in the 16th Century proposing unusual and controversial theories. He was a forerunner of Hahnemann and used the simillimum principle (like cures like suffering) and found specific relationships between plants and mineral remedies and disease symptoms.

> *"All that mankind needs for good health and healing is provided in nature, ... the challenge for science is to find it."*
>
> —*Paracelsus, Father of Pharmacology 1493-1541*

So, now Wheelwright enters the historical picture. As a chemist and biochemist, Wheelwright was very familiar with allopathic drug treatments. As a student of every healing system on the planet, he was well aware of the beautiful and profound principles of homeopathy. And, as a master herbalist he brought forth a new and unique dimension in both the treatment of imbalances and maintenance of vital health: in homeopathic terms, his formulas could be designated, "zero-x, mother-tincture, plant-combination sarcodes[14]," because they present the resonance of healthy tissue (a sarcode) along with the whole-herb nutritive support.

Here's the point. When a person is ill, there are generally two methods to restore health. One is allopathic which will attempt to get rid of the symptoms with toxic drugs that suppress the patient's vitality and ameliorate the presence and perception of symptoms. The other is homeopathic which will stimulate the patient's vitality to heal the cause of the symptoms and restore optimal health according to the principles of natural cure. However, Wheelwright pioneered a third method, one that is compatible with homeopathic treatment, and can be supportive of allopathic treatment.

---

[14] Sarcode (organotherapy) - a glandular or tissue extract made into a homeopathic remedy. When administered it acts to restore normal functioning of the respective tissue or organ by stimulating its normal function.

Discourse 4:
Neutral Healing

So where does Wheelwright's Systemic Herbology fit in? Well, generally, the bio-energetic applications of Systemic Formulas are homeopathic in that they are "like" the targeted tissue, but they are not "like suffering" (the like-pathos of homeopathy), so they do not really qualify as homeopathics. Rather than build his healing system on the negative suppression of symptoms (allopathy), or the positive stimulation of the vital force with an artificial disease energy (homeopathy), Wheelwright chose the neutral, balanced zone for his formulas. Hence the totally new dimension of Systemic Herbology.

Now we enter the neutral dimension of healing. And this dimension is compatible with both allopathy and homeopathy. It's not exclusive. Remember that Paracelsus taught both the homeopathic and neutral applications of herbs, so this is an extension of hundreds of years of healing evolution.

So when Systemic Formulas are used, they neither suppress symptoms like allopathic drugs, nor do they stimulate the vital force to react against them with an often-violent reaction or homeopathic 'aggravation'. They provide a balanced, gentle, nutritional influence to restore specific tissues to a more optimal health. But by no means think of Systemic Formulas as weak or benign. Their gentleness is based on a profound strength.

"Systemic Formulas are very powerful influences on the tissues, but the influence is a gentle nudge to balance, not to counterbalance."

— *A.S. Wheelwright, Odgen, UT, meeting with practitioners.*

In both the ancient and modern herbal traditions, herbs have most often been used to counterbalance a condition; though they can, in the hands of skilled practitioners (most often practitioners of Chinese herbal medicine), apply their focus to causes rather than effects. In Wheelwright's research, his formulas simply introduce balanced support of the tissue, regardless of the cause or effects of its symptoms. Then, in the Wheelwright Healing System, the practitioner can track down the deeper causes and comprehensively support the healing process in all its needed arenas.

"The doctors assistance in the healing process must cooperate with and follow the body's curative pathway to restore its most optimal and vibrant health."

—Wheelwright aphorism

Ch'i Lee's Challenge. In one of his early lectures in Dallas, Texas, Wheelwright was challenged by an elderly acupuncturist, Dr. Chi Lee (who got some mileage out of a chili pepper logo playing off his name) who did not initially understand the lecture. The elderly gentleman presented this argument. When Chi Lee provided Chinese medicinal treatment to a patient with heat in the kidneys, he gave herbs, along with his needle therapy, that cooled the kidneys and thus quickly restored the kidneys to balance. He challenged Wheelwright by saying that if he didn't counter heat with a cooling therapy, and if he used only a balanced Systemic formula, then the body's compromise would be somewhere between heat and normal, otherwise called "warm," and thus health would not be fully restored.

Wheelwright countered his argument by saying that his balanced formulas delivered a "hundred times balance" and were perfectly capable of restoring complete balance without running the risk of side effects or counterbalancing the kidneys which could result in new symptoms or additional stress on the system. After the lecture I attempted to further explain Doc's reply and came up with this "health scale analogy."

Here's another way to understand what Wheelwright was saying. Let's set up a scale for health that can go two ways, chronic and acute. Health is a balanced state so it is zero on the scale, the fulcrum. Health is neither too hot, nor too cold. It is neither too dry nor damp. It is neither fatigued nor overly energetic. A fever is represented here as +100 because it is a positive imbalance-response to a stimulus with caloric heat. On the other side of the scale, a chronic-degenerative disease is represented as -100 because it is a lack of vitality.

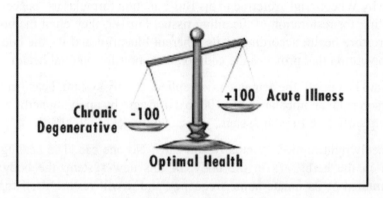

So, the classic herbal and allopathic approach is to attempt to treat a fever of +100 (positive 100) with a cooling therapy of -100 (negative 100) and thus the average is Zero (0) and optimal health is restored.

This seems good until we realize that the therapy, if prolonged, can overcompensate and cause an imbalance toward the chronic degenerative side, or more likely, cause various side effects of such a drastic approach. Nonetheless, this see-saw approach is how most herbal and allopathic therapies operate.

So the acupuncturist challenged Wheelwright saying, how can you treat a fever of +100 with a balanced formula of Zero (0), and not end up at +50 and still be sick, just less so? And Wheelwright's answer was, "my formulas provide a hundred times balance" meaning that the balancing factor was so strong it would help the body restore optimal health. The healing force was many times stronger than the disease response.

Thus, let's shift our analogy to a grading system for further clarity. If the fever is an F and the Systemic formula an A, then a simple average would indeed be a grade of C. But if the Systemic formula were a hundred A's, then despite the F, the grade average is an A.

So, how does Wheelwright get a hundred A's in his formulas? He does this because he designed his formulas bio-energetically. He formulated for synergism meaning that every ingredient adds to a sum greater than the total of the parts. As Wheelwright formulated, new electron shells of bio-energy automatically became part of the formula. Thus the power of the formula is that it provides the neutral, optimal, health resonance pattern with 'energy to spare' via the *bond* aspect with each dose. This is why Wheelwright referred to his Bio-Function formulas as "beacons" calling for restoration of the ailing tissue. Further, they elicit the body to restore health according to its inherent blueprint and it's the body's cooperation that provides the additional support for optimal health.

Not to be put off, the acupuncturist replied, "In my system, I can get the person from an imbalance of +100 to a true zero by applying herbs with energy of -100. In your system, you can only get to 99.99%."

Wheelwright replied, "Actually you can't. No one can. The healing is not in the herbs; it's in the body. In this new system, the body is reminded of its innate home frequency and it will restore itself to its most optimal health with the advantages (and despite any disadvantages) of the herbs. I'm not saying that the way you practice is not as good as this new system. Not at all. I have only the highest esteem for Chinese medicine. And, I'm not saying that I can get to the same place of restored health any faster than your system in this example. But in this example we're using, we are only talking about correcting an acute distress. I do maintain that, in general terms, this new system is more effective in building the integrity of the tissue and establishing a more dynamic, energetic state of health, and I honestly believe it is indeed faster for chronic conditions."

The acupuncturist and Wheelwright became good friends and we visited "The Chili Pepper Clinic" in Arlington, Texas twice during the next year to help with the applications of Wheelwright's formulas before Dr. Lee passed away. Dr. Lee often called Wheelwright's herbal formulas, "needles in capsules."

Wheelwright's research found that if he based his herbal formulations on the tissue resonance frequency, and constructed his formula for synergism, then the result was a balanced formula that had the energy to help the body restore balance and thus heal.

For practitioners of the natural healing arts, this means that Systemic Formulas are safe, gentle, and powerful allies of the body's innate healing processes, and compatible with many modalities of treatment including homeopathy and acupuncture.

Beyond being a third philosophical way to heal, Wheelwright taught that the formulas allow the tissue to restore and repair itself, and thus go beyond simple healing or alleviation of symptoms, and enter into a realm of more optimal function. Thus, as practitioners, we can go beyond simple restoration of health into health maintenance and optimal health function.

Because health is so much more than the mere absence of disease or the absence of symptoms, what about the positive, energetic side of the health scale—an area where there are no symptoms to guide a treatment? Health can be built toward even more ecstatic states where well-being predominates and the mind is clear and energetic. The legacy of Doc Wheelwright through his formulas is that we can be more than alleviators of symptoms. We can move into the arena of vitality enhancement far beyond the status quotient. Systemic Formulas give us the opportunity to support our health even when we are well so we can not only stay well, but we can continuously build our vitality for a more dynamic life.

Discourse 5:
Balance and The Bio-Command Directives

So now, with that historical perspective and philosophical insight thoroughly mastered, here's how
the Bio-Command formulas can assist our work
as natural health practitioners.

Balance in a tissue consists of several facets
including times of activation (the Chinese body
clock), building, cleansing, repairing, defending itself, and healing
itself. Balance is not a static state but a dynamic, cyclical inter-working
of the tissue's cells and bio-energy.

In a balanced system there is a time for the tissue's unique and different
priorities, each active in their own time within the various rhythms of
life.

The Bio-Function formula introduces herbs, cellular identity factors,
nutrients, and a balancing bio-energetic impulse to the body for the
normalization of a tissue and its system. Within the balanced cycle that
comprises a tissue's activities are six preoccupations—the six arenas
that the Bio-Command formulas address. The Bio-Command formulas
capitalize on a specific, inherent activity without disturbing the
balanced operation of the tissue or the formula designed to support that
tissue.

There are two triads of tissue processes: 1) the active "job description"
of the tissue defined by its cellular identity including activity, maintenance, and repair functions; and 2) the defense mechanisms to protect
the integrity of the tissue.

Here they are depicted:

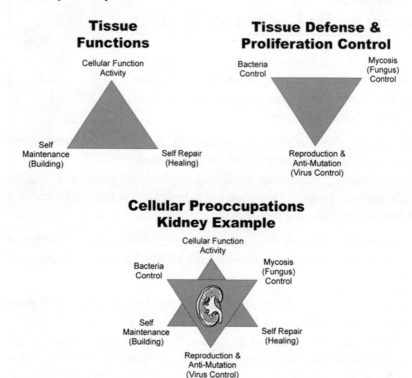

Tissue Functions

Cellular Function Activity

Self Maintenance (Building)

Self Repair (Healing)

Tissue Defense & Proliferation Control

Bacteria Control

Mycosis (Fungus) Control

Reproduction & Anti-Mutation (Virus Control)

Cellular Preoccupations Kidney Example

Cellular Function Activity

Bacteria Control

Mycosis (Fungus) Control

Self Maintenance (Building)

Self Repair (Healing)

Reproduction & Anti-Mutation (Virus Control)

Bio-Commands assist the cellular/tissue preoccupations. That's an important point so here it is again: The Bio-Command formula capitalizes on a specific inherent activity of balanced tissue activity without disturbing the balanced operation of that tissue.

The reason this is an important point is because some practitioners think that the Bio-Command inflicts a specific will upon the tissue in sort of an *"I now command thee, thyroid, to activate this instant"* approach if Gf (Thyroid) and #1 (Activator) were used. But this is not so. The activation of the thyroid does not push the thyroid out of balance. It cannot make it "hyper" or work when it is supposed to rest and repair itself. It only capitalizes on more optimal activation of the thyroid when it's time for the thyroid to activate and perform its responsibilities. This activation does not mean that the thyroid will fail to build or heal or stabilize itself because the #1 (Activator) formula is used.

However, if the thyroid is overactive, it does not make sense to support its activation with the #1 Activator because it is already, errantly over-activated. That would not be a constructive application of the formulas. Instead, the practitioner must look at what the cause of the over-activity is. Is it an over secretion of the pituitary's thyroid stimulating hormone? (If so, why?) An auto immune issue? (If so, what caused it?) An iodine toxicity? A thyroxin resistance at the cellular level? An issue with fatty acid metabolism? What?

Many practitioners have expressed opinions such as *"I'm afraid to use #1 (Activator) with Gf (Thyroid) because what if it over-stimulates the thyroid and I cause Grave's Disease?"* [Note: Grave's Disease is a chronically overactive or hyper thyroid.] But this is not possible in a balanced system. The Gf (Thyroid) formula is designed to balance and strengthen the thyroid as tissue. The #1 (Activator) will activate a better response when the meridian clock calls for the thyroid (and triple warmer) to function in balance with other endocrine glands. The inclusion of #1 (Activator) with the Gf (Thyroid) formula simply means that the thyroid will function more actively when it's supposed to be active than if the #1 (Activator) formula were not included.

Another way of saying this is: the thyroid will "thyroid" better, the kidneys will "kidney" better, the brain will "brain" better when supported by the appropriate Bio-Function Formula plus the #1 (Activator). This is because the #1 (Activator) enhances the tissues ability to perform its chief functions.

To include the other Bio-Command formulas in this current discussion, let's quickly review their purposes. The #2 (Builder) enhances the building mechanism. The #3 (Bactrex) enhances the anti-bacterial, immunological response. The #4 (FungDx) enhances the anti-fungal, immunological response. The #5 (Stabilizer) enhances the integrity, and prevents potential abnormal cellular development of mutated cells especially due to viral-initiated mutations. The #6 (Healer) enhances the quality of the deep repair function. Each Bio-Command must operate in cooperation with the overall balance of the body system.

The Bio-Command Formulas magnify the effect of the Bio-Function formula toward a specific area of tissue operation up to two to four times the original influence, thus capitalizing on better function within a balanced system.

By now, it should be clearly emphasized that use of the Bio-Command formulas enhances an aspect of balanced function, but do not and cannot push a tissue out of balance.

Now back to the practitioner with the Grave's Disease question. Does this mean that we will give Gf (Thyroid) and #1 (Activator) to a person with Grave's Disease? Probably not. At least not without first having the body prove it is no longer experiencing overactive thyroid activity. Why would we activate an overactive chief function? Instead we would choose other Bio-Commands such as #5 (Stabilizer) and #6 (Healer) to accompany Gf (Thyroid). But it is decisions such as these that are the domain of the doctor and natural health practitioner. And that's why Systemic Formulas are for professional use and direction and not sold in stores for public consumption.

The Bio-Command formulas allow the full impact of the Bio-Function formula, but strengthens one specific aspect. This is simply a way to bolster the weakest part of a tissue while simultaneously helping the whole tissue. For example, let's take some cases of miscellaneous health issues and exemplify each of the Bio-Command formulas. This way, we'll see how easy it is to 'mix-and-match' the formulas.

#1 (Activator)

- Hypo-thyroidism - we could use Gf (Thyroid) plus #1 (Activator). Such a program will still support the Thyroid in all its balanced aspects including building, tissue immunity, and healing any damage, but the #1 (Activator) will help the thyroid do its chief function of manufacturing viable thyroxin molecules from iodine with greater ease and certainty, thus helping correct the hypothyroid condition. Hypo-thyroidism often occurs with normal thyroid stimulating hormone (TSH) levels and is a thyroxin resistance at the cellular level. While science investigates this phenomenon, the application of the herbs is helpful to having the thyroid construct the proper, viable hormones and thyroxin-resistance is clinically correctable as evidenced by other metabolic activities.

- Sluggish memory - occurs when the information is learned, but the person has trouble accessing the information. Use B (Brain) to support the frontal lobe of the brain where the memory faculty is predominant, and add the #1 (Activator). Great before exams, and performances. Note: the #1 (Activator) supports the hypothalamus part of the brain specifically.

#2 (Builder)

- Weak kidneys after malnutrition (fast food diet) - we could use K (Kidney) plus #2 (Builder) to restore integrity to the kidney tissue. The K (Kidney) formula would still support the kidneys and renal system in all its balanced functions such as filtering the blood, providing vitamin D, maintaining electrolytes, regulating blood pressure, and so forth, as well as the other bioenergetic functions for normal kidney ch'i, but the much needed building or rebuilding work can now be enhanced and proper protein structures assembled to restore the kidneys tissue integrity.
- Weak, tired eyes - we simply focus the herbal nutrition of the I (Eye) formula that supports the eyes, the optic nerve, and the brain's vision center with the body's building and strengthening processes by adding the #2 (Builder).

#3 (Bactrex)

- Chronic Bronchitis - we could use R (Lung) plus #3 (Anti-Infective). The R (Lung) formula will still support the lungs in all balanced aspects including activation at the 3-5 a.m. meridian time, building as the cells need to rebuild, anti-fungal response, anti-abnormal cellular response, and healing, but with the #3 (Anti-Infective) formula, particular emphasis will be placed on the body's ability to destroy the detrimental bacteria, and thus the body is encouraged and supported to heal itself of chronic bronchitis. [Please note there are other applicable formulas including ATAK (Immune Rejuvenator), Gt (Thymus),and the Metal Tonify/Sedate formulas, but this is one, basic example.]
- Cystitis (Bladder Infection) - we could use Ks (Kidney-s) for support and targeting to the kidneys, ureter, bladder, and urethra, and add the #3 (Bactrex) to it for a specific anti-bacterial focus. Further enhance-

ment could come from the Gold (Immune Plus) formula and the Sedate Water formulas.

#4 (FungDx)

- Candida invasion of the intestinal lumen - we could use C (Colon) plus #4 (Corrector). The C (Colon) formula will provide balanced support to the colon as tissue, and with the help of the #4 (Corrector), candida can be eliminated and the tissue integrity restored. [Further, the use of the ENZEE (Anti-Pathogenic Enzymes) could help eliminate the Candida's supportive terrain and the ABC (Acidophilus, Bifidus, Bulgaricus) probiotic formula would be needed as well to restore beneficial culture.]
- Fungal mycosis of the lungs - use the R (Lung) formula for support to the lungs as a tissue. Add the #4 (FungDx) to the R (Lung) for specific emphasis on anti-fungal activities. Such a program should also be enhanced by the Wheelwright Healing System to include 1) constitutional support (Metal Tonify), and 2) drainage support with ACX (Vitamin Detox).

#5 (Stabilizer)

- Ovarian cyst - we could use F+ (Female Plus) along with #5 (Stabilizer). The F+ would still impart its hormonal balancing, adaptagenic nutrients and support of all aspects of the female endocrine system, and the #5 (Stabilizer) would direct a specific effort toward the normalization of the abnormal cellular growth. We would expect the body then to be able to reduce the cyst and finally resolve the cyst by absorption or discharge of the contents.
- Rectal Polyps - consider the hub of C (Colon) with #5 (Stabilizer). Then to that, add a constitutional element such as the General Sedate formula, and of course, correct the terrain with ACCELL.

#6 (Healer)

- Whiplash - we could use N3 (Nerve, Anti-Tensive) and #6 (Healer). Without compromising the full range of nerve support provided by the N-3 (Nerve, Anti-Tensive) formula that also can play an important role in overall nerve support, the #6 (Healer) specifically supports the trauma to the cervical nerve roots. Thus less pain and more rapid healing may result.

- <u>Post Anti-Parasitic Support</u> - after an anti-parasitic protocol such as VRM-1 for large worms, or VRM-3 for protozoa, giardia, and other microscopic parasites; it is a good time to focus on healing the damage to the colon tissue that was caused by the parasite-favorable terrain (alkaline pH, low fiber, poor diet), as well as the damage caused by the parasite(s). To that end, use C (Colon) and #6 (Healer) with a scoop of ACCELL. [Note: Accell and #6 together are premier to help the body heal 'leaky gut syndrome'.]

Conclusion

Bio-Command formulas provide a brilliant and powerful approach to the natural healing of the body. Practitioners who endeavor to master Systemic Herbology and The Wheelwright Healing System will find that the Bio-Command formulas provide a method for quicker, more thorough and more lasting results from the herbs—the natural and genuine medicines for health and healing.

The Bio-Command formulas provide the herbalist the ability to direct the effects of balanced herbal nutrition to accomplish a specific nutritional goal by its interaction with the targeted tissue.

When taken together, Bio-Command Formulas combine with Bio-Function Formulas to direct them to a specific purpose.

Properly designed combination formulas are far superior to using individual herbs in most instances. When compatible herbs are combined, they can help enhance the healing effects many times, like a marriage, where the two are greater than the sum total of one plus one. This is called "synergism." Further, properly combined herbs help reduce the inherent side effects of individual herbs, thus making the resulting formula more safe and effective.

Afterword

The Legacy Continues: Systemic Formulas in the 21st Century

In 1984, Doc Wheelwright's son, Stuart, Jr., launched Systemic Formulas, Inc. a company dedicated to the procurement, preservation, storage, design, manufacture, and marketing of his father's herbal research and formulas; as well as advancing the Systemic Wellness Philosophy in all its multifaceted arenas. In the last six years of his life, Doc Wheelwright taught his son the meticulous and precise formula-making process.

Stu Wheelwright, Jr.

To accommodate the many facets and operations required of the specialized manufacturing process, Stu, Jr. built the Systemic Formulas building in Odgen, Utah. Here, the herbal and nutritional ingredients are inspected, evaluated, and stored so they can be used the formula-production process. Over the years, Stu, Jr. has built a modern manufacturing facility so that every aspect of quality control can be maintained under one roof.

Doc Wheelwright's formulation process is quite extensive. Different components of his formulations are assembled in a precise "recipe" before they are ready for the final mixing and preparation for being capsulated, or made into tinctures or extracts. Some ingredients are combined, ground together and allowed to dry to a specified consistency; others are mixed and stirred, and others combined in a predetermined order. Doc Wheelwright provided exacting standards about how the formulas must be constructed to derive the bio-energetic and biochemical benefits.

Systemic Formulas, Ogden, UT

Herbs in storage

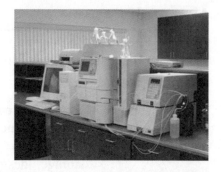

A key feature of the Systemic facility is the state-of-the-art microbiology laboratory where the herbs can be assayed to ensure they are the correct genus and species, as well as tested to ensure they are safe regarding contaminants and pathogenic organisms.

Keeping pace with modern research and the demands of the nutritional healing industry, Stu, Jr. has brought out several new formulations in the Wheelwright tradition. The two most prominent formulations are the ACCELL formula that addresses the bio-terrain of the healing triad (the digestion, the colon, and the liver); and the ENZEE formula

Giant mixers that make the ACCELL formula—a formula with over 70 ingredients

which uses enzymes to clean up the extra-cellular carbohydrate sludge that forms a breeding ground for candida, mycosis, pathogenic bacteria, and virus.

Dr. Dayeoon Kim

The operations of Systemic Formulas, Inc. is conducted by General Manager, Dr. Dayeoon Kim, who provides a scientific background with first-hand knowledge of medicinal herbs. Dr. Kim provides management expertise to all facets of the daily operations of running an innovative formulary and manufacturing facility.

Doc Wheelwright's daughter, Launa Morris, serves as Controller for Systemic Formulas, Inc. and works with her brother, Stu, Jr., to perpetuate the Wheelwright Legacy by providing a sound business structure.

Systemic Formulas, Inc. is dedicated to providing Health Professionals the support they need to make nutritional herbology and the Wheelwright Legacy the premier natural healing modality in the 21st Century.

The Systemic Wellness Vision. *Systemic Formulas is dedicated to being a recognized leader in nutritional wellness based upon principles of integrity, quality, safety, and honesty ultimately leading to the Systemic Wellness Lifestyle.*

—Stu Wheelwright, Jr.

Appendix A

Bio-Command Protocols

Here are some general protocols to exemplify how the Bio-Command formulas play an important role in programming more successful nutritional support. In these examples, we will move through a rotation of the Bio-Command formulas to exemplify the ability to change the program while holding constant with the overall theme. This is the ultimate art of the Bio-Command applications as the thorough support of a tissue over time allows the body time to establish a tissue integrity, a new terrain and a new homeostasis.

Kidney Toning Wellness Program

General, nutritional support for people with:

- A history of nephritis
- A history of kidney stones
- Chronic low back pain
- Resistance to detoxification (needs drainage support)
- Tendency to water retention

Bio Function +	Bio Command +	Dragon Rising +	Bio Challenge	Frequency/ Duration
2 Ks (Kidney S)	2 #3 (Bactrex)	2 Water Sedate	1 KDIR (Fluidren)	a.m. 15 days
2 K (Kidney)	2 #3 (Bactrex)	2 Water Sedate	1 KDIR (Fluidren)	p.m. 15 days
Then				
2 Ks (Kidney S)	2 #5 (Stabilizer)	2 Water Tonify	2 KDIR (Fluidren)	bid 15 days
Then				
2 K (Kidney)	1 #2 (Builder)	Water Tonify	1 KDIR (Fluidren)	bid 15 days
Then				
2 K (Kidney)	1 #1 (Activator)			a.m. 15 days
2 Ks (Kidney-S)				p.m. 15 days

Supplies Needed:

- K (Kidney). . . . . . 120 caps . . . . .2 bottles
- Ks (Kidney-S) . . . 120 caps . . . . .2 bottles
- KDIR (Fluidren). . 120 caps . . . . .2 bottles
- Water Sedate . . . . . 60 caps . . . . .1 bottle
- Water Tonify . . . . . 60 caps . . . . .1 bottle
- #3 (Bactrex). . . . . . 60 caps . . . . .1 bottle
- #5 (Stabilizer). . . . 30 caps . . . . .1 bottle
- #2 (Builder) . . . . . . 30 caps . . . . .1 bottle
- #1 (Activator). . . . . 30 caps . . . . .1 bottle

Complimentary Formulas
- Ga (Adrenal)
- Hcv (Heart/Cardiovascular)

Hypo-Thyroid Toning Wellness Program

General nutrition for people who are:

- Sluggish on arising
- On the elevated side of the TSH (Thyroid Stimulating Hormone) range per blood lab report
- Cold natured (cold hands and feet), lack vital heat
- Gain weight or have inability to loose weight
- Hypoglycemic (Note: will add Ps and additional Ga to program)
- Experience pre-menstrual syndrome (Note: will add F+, Fpms, Ls to program)
- Mis-manufacturing the thyroxin molecule (toxic thyroxin, thyroxin resistance)
- Have Chronic Fatigue Syndrome or Fibro-myalgia

Bio Function	+	Bio Command	+	Adjunctive Support	Frequency/Duration
2 Gf (Thyroid)		1 #1 (Activator)		2 Gb (Pituitary)	tid for 10 days
Then					
2 Gf (Thyroid)		1 #2 (Builder)		1 Gb (Pituitary)	bid for 10 days
Then					
2 Gf (Thyroid)		1 #5 (Stabilizer)		1 Gb (Pituitary)	bid for 10 days
Then					
2 Gf (Thyroid)		1 #6 (Restore)		1 Gb (Pituitary)	bid for 10 days
Then					
2 Gf (Thyroid)		1 #2 (Builder)		2 Ga (Adrenal)	tid for 10 days

Supplies Needed:

- Gf (Thyroid). . . . . 240 caps . . . . .4 bottles
- Gb (Pituitary). . . . 120 caps . . . . .2 bottles
- Ga (Adrenal) . . . . . 60 caps . . . . .1 bottle
- #1 (Activator). . . . 30 caps . . . . .1 bottle
- #2 (Builder) . . . . . . 50 caps . . . . .2 bottles
- #5 (Stabilizer). . . . 30 caps . . . . .1 bottle
- #6 (Restore) . . . . . . 30 caps . . . . .1 bottle

Complimentary Formulas:

- F+ (Female)
- M+ (Super Male +)
- Gt (Thymus)
- Earth Sedate

Brain Building Program

General nutrition for people who experience:

- Memory Lapses
- Forgetfulness
- Brain fog
- Confusion
- Absent mindedness
- Low test scores in school after learning the material

For the first 2 weeks start with the "Brain Build" triad of 2-B (Brain) + 2-I (Eye) + 2-Gb (Pituitary) bid, then continue with just the B (Brain) formula as the Bio-Function component, as follows. Note: the adjunctive support slot allows the practitioner to chose other enhancing formulas and covers a wide range of nutritional support. Here's how:

Bio Function	+	Bio Command	+	Adjunctive Support	Frequency/Duration
2 B (Brain)		2 I (Eye)		2 Gb (Pituitary)	bid for 14 days
Then					
2 B (Brain)		1 #2 (Builder)		3 LEV (Lecithin)	bid for 14 days
Then					
2 B (Brain)		1 #6 (Healer)		3 LEV (Lecithin)	bid for 14 days
Then					
1 B (Brain)		1 #1 (Activator)		2 LEV (Lecithin)	bid for 14 days
Then					
2 B (Brain)		1 #2 (Builder)		2 BFO (Borage/ Flax/Fish Oil)	bid for 14 days

Bio Function	+	Bio Command	+	Adjunctive Support	Frequency/Duration
Then					
2 B (Brain)		1 #6 (Healer)		2 BFO (Borage/ Flax/Fish Oil)	bid for 14 days
Then					
1 B (Brain)		1 #1 (Activator)		2 BFO (Borage/ Flax/Fish Oil)	bid for 14 days

Supplies Needed:

- B (Brain) . . . . 294 caps . . . . .5 bottles
- LEV (Lecithin) . . . 196 caps . . . . .2 bottles
- BFO (Borage/
  Flax/Fish Oil) . . . . 168 caps . . . . .3 bottles
- #1 (Activator) . . . . . 56 caps . . . . .2 bottles
- #2 (Builder) . . . . . . 56 caps . . . . .2 bottles
- #6 (Builder) . . . . . . 56 caps . . . . .2 bottles

Heart Building Program

General nutrition for people who:

- Have heart concerns
- Have not exercised (couch potatoes) and are just beginning to exercise
- Want to strengthen their heart for longevity
- Have a history of heart issues

As preparation for the program and to become accustomed to herbal support, for the first two weeks, take 1 H (Heart) and 2 Hcv (Heart/Cardiovascular) with breakfast and supper. Then follow this program and note that only the Bio-Command changes:

Bio Function	+	Bio Command	+	Adjunctive Support	Frequency/Duration
2 H (Heart)		1 #6 (Healer)		2 Hcv (Heart/Cardiovascular) 1 MIN (Multi Minerals) 1 BFO (Borage/Flax/Fish Oil) 1 EZV (Natural Vitamin E)	*bid* 14 days

Then

| 2 H (Heart) | | 1 #2 (Builder) | | 2 Hcv (Heart/Cardiovascular) 1 MIN (Multi Minerals) 1 BFO (Borage/Flax/Fish Oil) 1 EZV (Natural Vitamin E) | *bid* 14 days |

Then

| 2 H (Heart) | | 2 #3 (Bactrex) | | 2 Hcv (Heart/Cardiovascular) | *bid* 14 days |

Bio Function	+	Bio Command	+	Adjunctive Support	Frequency/Duration
				1 MIN (Multi Minerals) 1 BFO (Borage/Flax/Fish Oil) 1 EZV (Natural Vitamin E)	

Then

Bio Function	+	Bio Command	+	Adjunctive Support	Frequency/Duration
2 H (Heart)		2 #4 (FungDx)		2 Hcv (Heart/ Cardiovascular) 1 MIN (Multi Minerals) 1 BFO (Borage/Flax/Fish Oil) 1 EZV (Natural Vitamin E)	*bid* 14 days

Then

Bio Function	+	Bio Command	+	Adjunctive Support	Frequency/Duration
2 H (Heart)		1 #5 (Stabilizer)		2 Hcv (Heart/ Cardiovascular) 1 MIN (Multi Minerals) 1 BFO (Borage/Flax/Fish Oil) 1 EZV (Natural Vitamin E)	*bid* 14 days

Then

Bio Function	+	Bio Command	+	Adjunctive Support	Frequency/Duration
2 H (Heart)		1 #1 (Activator)		2 Hcv (Heart/ Cardiovascular) 1 MIN (Multi Minerals) 1 BFO (Borage/Flax/Fish Oil) 1 EZV (Natural Vitamin E)	*bid* 14 days

ADHD (Attention Deficit Hyperactivity Disorder) Program

General, nutritional support for people with:

- Attention Deficit Disorder
- Hyperactive tendencies
- Difficulty focusing in school
- Restlessness at school
- Learning difficulties

Note 1: This program focuses on four ADHD-related issues: 1) Nourishment and support of the brain and nerves; 2) Heavy metal detoxification; 3) Anti-parasitic support; and 4) Essential fatty acid nutrition.

Note 2: Most Systemic formulas come in liquid forms as well as capsules. This program makes use of several Systemic formulas in liquid form (concentrated extracts denoted as "CX") so they are easy to administer to children.

Note 3: The "dps" designation refers to "drops" of the liquid extracts.

Bio Function	+	Bio Command	+	Dragon Rising	+	Bio Challenge	+	Bio Nutrient
With Breakfast								
3 dps cxB (Brain) 3 dps cxI (Eye) 3 dps cxN (Nerve)		3 dps cx2 (Builder)		2 Fire Sedate		3 dps cxVRM-1 3 dps cxVRM-3		2 BFO (Borage/ Flax/ Fish Oil)
After School								
3 dps cxB (Brain) 3 dps cxN (Nerve)		3 dps cx2 (Builder)		1 Fire Sedate 1 Earth Sedate		3 dps cxCLNZ 3 dps cxACX		

Bio Function	+	Bio Command	+	Dragon Rising	+	Bio Challenge	+	Bio Nutrient
With Supper								
3 dps cxB (Brain) 3 dps cxI (Eye) 3 dps cxN (Nerve)		3 dps cx2 (Builder)		2 Earth Sedate		3 dps cxVRM-1 3 dps cxVRM-3		2 BFO (Borage/ Flax/ Fish Oil)

Liquid formulas can be mixed with each other in a few ounces of juice or water.

After two weeks on the Bio-Command #2 (Builder), switch to Bio-Command #5 (Stabilizer), then at two-week intervals change the Bio-Command to #4 (FungDx), then 3# (Bactrex), then #6 (Healer), then #1 (Activator).

Supplies Needed For 30-Day Program:

CX B (Brain)....... 1/2 oz. ....1 bottle
CX I (Eye)........ 1/2 oz. ....1 bottle
CX N (Nerve) ...... 1/2 oz. ....1 bottle
CX 2 (Builder)...... 1/2 oz. ....1 bottle
CX VRM-1 .... 1/2 oz. ....1 bottle
CX VRM-3 .... 1/2 oz. ....1 bottle
Fire Sedate .... 90 caps ....1.5 bottles
Earth Sedate .... 90 caps ....1.5 bottles
BFO (Borage/
Flax Fish Oil) ...... 60 caps ....2 bottles

Liver Support Program

General, nutritional support for or people with:

- Concern for their liver health
- Elevated liver enzymes (ALT, AST)
- Poor digestion
- Hepatitis
- A need for better detoxification

Here we move through the Bio-Command formulas with comprehensive Chinese 5-Element and Bio-Challenge formulas that support the liver at the deep, cellular level.

Bio Function +	Bio Command +	Dragon Rising +	Bio Challenge +	Frequency/ Duration
1scoop ACCELL in juice or water before breakfast throughout the program.				
2 Ls (Liver-S)	2 #3 (Bactrex)	2 Wood Tonify	1 OXAA (Organizer Cell)	a.m. 15 days
2 L (Liver)	2 #3 (Bactrex)	2 Wood Sedate	1 OXAA (Organizer Cell)	p.m. 15 days
Then				
2 Ls (Liver-S)	1 #5 (Stabilizer)	2 Wood Tonify	1 OXAA (Organizer Cell)	a.m. 15 days
2 L (Liver)	1 #5 (Stabilizer)	2 Wood Sedate	1 OXAA (Organizer Cell)	p.m. 15 days
Then				
2 Ls (Liver-S)	2 #4 (FungDx)	2 Wood Tonify	1 OXAA (Organizer Cell)	a.m. 15 days
2 L (Liver)	2 #4 (FungDx)	2 Wood Sedate	1 OXAA (Organizer Cell)	p.m. 15 days

Bio Function +	Bio Command +	Dragon Rising +	Bio Challenge +	Frequency/ Duration
Then				
2 Ls (Liver-S)	1 #6 (Healer)	2 Wood Tonify	1 DSIR (Intergen)	a.m. 15 days
2 L (Liver)	1 #6 (Healer)	2 Wood Sedate	1 DSIR (Intergen)	p.m. 15 days
Then				
2 Ls (Liver-S)	1 #2 (Builder)	2 Wood Tonify	1 DSIR (Intergen)	a.m. 15 days
2 L (Liver)	1 #2 (Builder)	2 Wood Sedate	1 DSIR (Intergen)	p.m. 15 days
Then				
2 Ls (Liver-S)	1 #1 (Activator)	2 Wood Tonify	1 OXAA (Organizer Cell)	a.m. 15 days
2 L (Liver)	1 #1 (Activator)	2 Wood Tonify	1 OXAA (Organizer Cell)	p.m. 15 days

Supplies Needed For 90-Day Program:

```
ACCELL . . . . . . . . . . . . canister . . . . . . . . .3 canisters
L (Liver) . . . . . . . . . . . 180 caps  . . . . . . . .3 bottles
Ls (Liver-S) . . . . . . . . . 180 caps  . . . . . . . .3 bottles
DSIR (Intergen)  . . . . . 120 caps  . . . . . . . .2 bottles
Wood Sedate . . . . . . . . 180 caps  . . . . . . . .3 bottles
Wood Tonify . . . . . . . . 180 caps  . . . . . . . .3 bottles
OXAA (Intergen) . . . . . 180 caps  . . . . . . . .3 bottles
#3 (Bactrex) . . . . . . . . . . 60 caps  . . . . . . . .1 bottle
#5 (Stabilizer . . . . . . . . . 30 caps  . . . . . . . .1 bottle
#2 (Builder) . . . . . . . . . . 30 caps  . . . . . . . .1 bottle
#1 (Activator) . . . . . . . . 30 caps  . . . . . . . .1 bottle
#4 (FungDx) . . . . . . . . . 60 caps  . . . . . . . .1 bottle
#6 (Healer) . . . . . . . . . . . 30 caps  . . . . . . . .1 bottle
```

Female Wellness Program (Menopause, Menses)

General nutrition for women who with:

- Menopausal initiated symptoms (insomnia, depression, fatigue)
- Hot flashes
- Menstrual cramping
- Skin eruptions before menses
- Excessive or clotted menstrual flow

This program supports the female endocrine system comprehensively. It can be enhanced with the Breast Lymphatic Massage (see: Breast Health at www.apple-a-daypress.com).

Bio Function +	Bio Command +	Adjunctive Support	Frequency/Duration
1 F+ (Female Plus) 1 Fpms (Fem Health)	1 #1 (Activator)	1 Gf (Thyroid) 1 Gb (Pituitary)	tid, for 10 days
Then			
2 F+ (Female Plus) 1 Fpms (Fem Health)	1 #2 (Builder)	1 Gf (Thyroid) 1 Ga (Adrenal)	tid, for 10 days
Then			
1 F+ (Female Plus) 1 Fpms (Fem Health)	1 #6 (Activator)	1 Gf (Thyroid) 1 Gb (Pituitary)	tid, for 10 days
Then			
2 F+ (Female Plus) 1 Fpms (Fem Health)	2 #4 (FungDx)	1 Gf (Thyroid) 1 Ga (Adrenal)	tid, for 10 days

Bio Function +	Bio Command +	Adjunctive Support	Frequency/Duration
Then			
2 F+ (Female Plus)	1 #5 (Stabilizer)	1 Gf (Thyroid)	tid, for 10 days
1 Fpms (Fem Health)		1 Gb (Pituitary)	
Then			
2 F+ (Female Plus)	1 #3 (Bactrex)	1 Gf (Thyroid)	tid, for 10 days
1 Fpms (Fem Health)		1 Ga (Adrenal)	
		1 Gb (Pituitary)	

Note: Formulas can be taken with meals.

Supplies Needed For 60-Day Program:

F+ (Female Plus) . . . . 360 caps . . . . . .6 bottles
Fpms (Female Health) . . . . 180 caps . . . . . .3 bottles
Gf (Thyroid) . . . . 180 caps . . . . . .3 bottles
Gb (Pituitary). . . . . 120 caps . . . . . .2 bottles
Ga (Adrenal) . . . . 120 caps . . . . . .2 bottles
#1 (Activator), ... 30 caps . . . . . .1 bottle
#2 (Builder) . . . . 30 caps . . . . . .1 bottle
#5 (Stabilizer) . . . . 30 caps . . . . . .1 bottle
#6 (Restore). . . . . 30 caps . . . . . .1 bottle
#4 (FungDX) . . . . 60 caps . . . . . .1 bottle

Appendix B

Guide to the Systemic Bio-Function Formulas
Featuring commentary on applications of the similar formulas.

The Bio-Function Formulas are nutritional support that concentrate on specific organs, glands, or gender processes. Formulated so as to balance needed factors and chelated with herbs, the Bio-Function formulas rebuild, re-educate, support, and provide effective but gentle relief for many wellness challenges.

#12 - B - BRAIN

This formula provides essential nutrients that promote concentration, clarity of thought, alertness and improved general memory functions. It supplies fourteen essential brain nutrients helping bridge the gap between the left and right hemispheres of the brain assuring greater mental power. Formula B helps combat brain dysfunction including hyperkinesias, border line I.Q., balancing high I.Q. people by supplying nutriments for neuron junctures. Formula B works well with Formulas I (Eye) and Gb (Pituitary); it is excellent for hyperactive children.

#14 - C - COLON

This formula assists in toning the bowel tissue and supports peristalsis and its effect as a hydrogogue (the ability to draw water into the colon). Formula C, programming of colon function, is a natural, non-gripping formula that builds and heals the colon and softens the stool; it flushes pollutants out of the lower colon.

#17 - D - DIGEST

Provides a *self-limiting*, enzyme solution that promotes digestion of proteins, carbohydrates, and fats. A broad spectrum digestive support formula that promotes proper levels of digestive acids and enzymes. This formula has three primary uses: 1) Use with food for broad, digestive benefits. 2) Use between meals to breakdown undigested protein artifacts. 3) Build the stomach's inherent digestive abilities, particularly the parietal cell's ability to make hydrochloric acid.

#18 - Ds - DIGEST S

This formula utilizes vegetable enzymes to provide support for good digestive health. It is particularly appropriate for people who experience bloating from cruciferous vegetables such as cabbage and mustard. Considered a milder version of the D Digestive formula, it is effective for those who have sensitive or irritated stomach conditions. Helps with the digestive function so the stomach can rest and rebuild its inherent vitality and function.

> **D versus Ds**
> *Use D when you want to re-build and strengthen the stomach's digestive faculties. Use Ds when you want to help the stomach perform its digestive functions better.*

#22 - F+ - FEMALE PLUS

This formula is considered to be the ultimate in providing nutritional support for healthy female biochemistry, hormonal balance and ovarian health. It greatly alleviates problems associated with the regulation of menstrual rhythms. Being an adaptagenic formula, it smoothes out the highs and lows to normalize the female menstrual cycle thus regulating and assisting it to achieve a healthy hormonal balance.

24 - Fpms - FEMALE HEALTH

Support for normal Female Cycles. It supports the entire female hormonal endocrine system including the thyroid by providing nutritional factors that aid in providing normal menstrual cycles as well as alleviating the excessive bleeding, hot flashes, mood swings and accompanying cramps.

> **F+ versus Fpms**
> *Use F+ to support the entire female hormonal system. Use Fpms when pre-menses symptoms predominate. Both formulas may be used in the same program.*

#31 - Ga - ADRENAL

The great body chemistry (pH) balancing formula that provides adrenal gland support and added energy. Ga supports the entire endocrine function, enhances energy and adrenals. Through providing support for the entire adrenal glands, (medulla and cortex), this formula supports the body's fundamental energy process.

#32 - Gb - PITUITARY / PINEAL

This formula provides nutritional support for all the important brain glands - pituitary, pineal and thalamus. It influences a healthy mental clarity and focus. It's useful in managing healthy fat utilization by the body, helps regulate the appetite, and re-establishes proper pituitary/pineal function including normalizing circadian rhythm as well as assisting in jetlag, head injuries and menopause.

#39 - Gf - THYROID

Builds and balances the thyroid gland; helps adjust changes due to environmental changes. This formula supports the thyroid glands' abilities as a master control gland in producing a normal, healthy metabolism. Often useful in both hypo as well as hyper thyroid responses, Gf assists the major metabolic actions of the endocrine systems. Helpful for promoting weight loss and in combating jet lag.

#41 - Gt - THYMUS

The Immune System Stabilizer - This formula effectively strengthens the body's innate immune systems; it balances and rebuilds the Thymus, strengthens weak muscles, tissues and bones. Used on a daily basis, Gt assists the body to resisting colds and influenza.

#44 - H - HEART

Rebuilds and normalizes essential heart functions. This formula supplies essential substances for healthy heart functions; helps maintain and rebuild the heart.

#45 - Hcv - HEART CARDIOVASCULAR

Nutritionally provides support for healthy blood functions including its inherent endocrine functions. Hcv supports the heart, the vessel system of the body and the lymphatic system. It assists in cleansing the lymphatic duct tissues.

#50 - I - EYES

Relieves eye stress, eye strain and reduces eye fatigue. - Supports the brain's optic center; supplies nutrients necessary for clear vision. It is indicated for use for students, older people, those who do "close" work, and for diabetics. Formula I assures the availability of necessary vitamin A as well as additional sight factors needed for good vision systems. Nutriments in this formula help strengthen muscles and tissues associated with good vision.

#56 - K - KIDNEY

Rehabilitates and modulates over-stressed kidneys. This formula stabilizes kidney functions. This is the preeminent kidney support formula for regulating pH, purifying and filtering the blood/lymph and maintaining electrolyte balance. It supports proper kidney functions and cleansing of kidney tissues. Used for supporting weak kidneys & normalizing blood pressure.

#58 - Ks - KIDNEY S

Stabilizes kidney functions - A variation of the K Kidney Formula that specializes in proper self cleaning mechanism often chosen for drainage support during cleansing programs, Ks is a more gentle version if the K formula is a cleanser itself. It is effective in reducing lower back pain and relieving the body of excess water without the loss of electrolytes. A specific in kidney programs if there is sand in the urine.

> *K versus Ks*
> *Use K to build the quality of the kidney tissue. Use Ks to encourage the kidneys to do the job better.*

#60 - L - LIVER

Support for the body's biochemical factory. This formula provides nutrition for the liver and gall bladder including softening, restoration, and rebuilding of the liver. This is the preeminent liver building formula that encourages regeneration of the liver's intercellular tissues. It assists with digestion and metabolism of macro nutrients.

#61 - Lb - LIVER/ GALL BLADDER

This formula helps establish proper portal duct function. It assists in purifying the blood of mucus forming matter, thins the congestion from the blood and is often used for hemorrhoids. Often effective with hyperactivity by relieving portal vein congestion. Particularly useful for those who have gall bladder colic.

#62 - Ls - LIVER S

Magnifies the liver's detoxification function; Ls stimulates health through a hepatic chelation and elimination processes. This formula supports detoxification and drainage including cytochrome p450 processes.

> ### L versus Ls and Lb
> Use L to focus on building the liver function (which results in better detoxification). Use Ls to support the liver's inherent cleansing activity. Use both L and Ls in a program, best at separate times. Lb's primary focus is the gall bladder and portal vein but it also provides general tonification to the liver.

#70 - M+ - MALE PLUS

Supports male glandular and endocrine systems, this formula provides vitality and energy while also increasing overall circulation and endurance. Promotes healthy libido and is useful for strength training, depression and male menopause.

#72 - Mpc - PROSTATA CORRECTOR

The premier prostate problem corrector and support formula - This formula provides nutrition that encourages a healthy prostate gland and provides a feeling of well being. Its specific nutritional focus helps overcome candida and helps to reduce congestion, inflammation swelling while promoting enhanced circulation.

#73 - Mpr - PROSTATA/OVATUM

Support for both the prostate and ovaries. This formula provides essential fatty acids for feeding, softening, and lubricating the prostate and feeding the ovaries. It enhances libido. It helps in the elasticity of the body's overall tissues thus being essential support for dry skin and nourishes synovial fluid.

> **Mpc versus Mpr**
> *Both formulas support the prostate gland from different positions—Mpc is therapeutic and Mpr is nutritionally supportive—and are often used together for a comprehensive support program.*

#74 - N - NERVE

General nerve support as well as bundle branch support. This formula assists in assuring healthy triglyceride levels in the cardiovascular system. N provides essential support for the bundle branch (right and left) system that carries a heavy electric load every moment of your life. It also is effective in repair and restoration of the nervous system in general; it helps strengthen damaged or frayed nerves. It is the premier nerve support formula for the bundle branch and the entire nervous system; it is extremely helpful in coping with nerve damage or when regeneration is a required factor. In many ways, N operates as a Bio-Command formula for nerve support to other organs.

#75 - N3 - RELAXA

A general pain reliever, it provides nutrients that calm frayed nerves. This is an all-natural, chemically-free, non toxic formula for the support of pain relief. It is a super nervine formula effective in promoting sleep and aiding in general relaxation. It is absolutely non habit forming and may provide the fulcrum for helping to alleviate any drug dependence. (Sleeping pills, chemical tranquilizers). Also, works well with Formula Ga in coping with chronic acidosis (the urine's pH value indicates acidity).

#77 - Nc - Calm

This formula provides relaxation from stress; it also provides a feeling of wellness. Designed to calm frayed nerves without any sedative effects, Nc nutritionally supports nerves and provides needed calcium as well as other important nerve support ingredients.

#78 - P PANCREAS

Builds and strengthens pancreatic functions including enzyme functions & normal functions (insulin & glucagons). It performs as a pancreas builder and nutritionally supports pancreatic functions by helping rebuild and restructure the pancreas itself.

#79 - Ps - PANCREAS S

Bolsters and maintains internal pancreatic balance and specifically helps normalize blood glucose. This formula supports a healthy pancreas and helps modulate glucose capacity for both hypo and hyper conditions.

> **P versus Ps**
> *Use P to support the pancreas as an entire tissue; and Ps when hypo- or hyper-glycemia issues are predominant.*

#80 - R LUNG

Master builder and a cleanser for the respiratory system. This formula supports a healthy respiratory system and maintains normal mucus levels; It increases the oxygen carrying capacity of the lungs. It may assist in easing respiratory dysfunction, emphysema, chronic sore throat, breathing impairment, smoker's cough, and hoarseness. Based upon the Lung-Thymus-Pancreas Triad, it utilizes a nutritional, herbal and broader spectrum approach for any respiratory imbalances.

#82 - S SPLEEN

Rebuilds the spleen - This formula nutritionally supports spleen health which can influence the lymph and blood systems as well as normalize the immune system. This is the foremost spleen support formula in western nutrition that produces consistent results.

Appendix C

The Bio-Challenge Formulas (Plus Other Wheelwright/Systemic Formulations)

Doc Wheelwright created a category of formulas called "Bio-Challenge" as precise herbal/nutritional support for specific health issues. These formulas add a uniquely-effective dimension to programs that focus on key concerns that are particularly relevant to humanity's current health challenges. Their specific, therapeutic support is one of the elements of the Wheelwright Healing System to consider when designing a healing program.

Here, with Bio-Challenge formulas, the practitioner finds powerful support for issues such as:

- pH (Acid /Alkaline balance)
- Arthritis
- Cleansing Mutated Micro-organisms
- Heavy Metal Cleansing
- Digestive relief and healing
- Anti-Bacterial, Acute
- Anti-Viral, Acute
- Kidney Cleansing
- Muscle Support
- Deep Cellular Cleansers
- Lymphatic Cleanser
- Anti-Parasitics

The Bio-Challenge formulas are often combined with Bio-Function formulas for an added dimension of therapeutic activity. And when applicable, a Bio-Command formula is combined for comprehensive support and program flexibility.

Let's look at some examples to see how the Bio-Challenge formulas play a critical role in the Wheelwright Healing System.

Example 1: Liver with Flukes and Candida

Challenge: The practitioner is concerned that the patient's liver is being affected by 1) liver flukes, and 2) Candida (yeast/fungus) involvement. If the parasites are removed, then the candida can become more prolific. If the candida is addressed, the parasites may proliferate.

Solution: Design a program based on the Wheelwright Healing System for:

- The constitutional state, use: Wood Tonify to support the liver/blood/kidney-yin
- Tissue support, targeting, and bio-energetic support, use: L (Liver) + Ls (Liver-s)
- Flukes and other migrating parasites, use: VRM-4 (Cell).
- The fundamental terrain of the liver, use: ACCELL for it's massive detoxification support.
- Candida: use Bio-Command #4 (FungDx)
- The underlying terrain that allows candida: use ENZEE (Metabolizing Enzyme Complex)

Now let's look at the seven elements of the Wheelwright Healing System and see how our comprehensive program supports the entire gamut of issues in this case.

Liver Flukes with Candida Involvement

Healing System Factor	Formulas That Address It
1. Constitutional support	Wood Tonify
2. Tissue biochemistry and integrity	L(Liver) + Ls (Liver -s)
3. Tissue nourishment	ACCELL
4. Pathogen involvements	VRM-4 (Cell), #4 (FungDX)
5. pH (terrain)	ACCELL
6. Drainage	ACCELL
7. Bio-Command Directive	#4 (FungDX)

Analysis. In this program, we have therapies from four formula categories (Bio-Command, Bio-Function, Bio-Basic, and Bio-Challenge teaming up to address the seven facets of the Wheelwright Healing System. And it's easy to see why this program is so effective—it addresses the entire, multifaceted and complex body processes that must cooperate for success.

Further, the practitioner has the ability to make periodic changes by examining other options such as introducing a different Bio-Command formula.

Example 2: Arthritic Inflammation of Joints with Lymphatic Congestion

Challenge: The arthritic inflammation is based on micro-parasites and is complicated by lymphatic congestion which sets the stage for aggravation during the cleansing process and thus failure of patient to comply with the program.

Solution: Let's design a simple program that gets to the primary issue, and then expand it for a full, comprehensive program.

Primary Issue	Formulas That Address It
1. Arthritis	ARTA (Jointez)
2. Micro-Parasites	VRM-2 (Small)
3. Lymphatic Congestion	SENG (Lymphogin)

Analysis: Here we apply three Bio-Challenge Formulas to focus on the three specific issues involved. The ARTA formula is a classic arthritis formula enhanced with anti-parasitic components. The VRM-2 is designed to help the body eliminate micro-parasites that travel in the blood and lymph and get in the extra cellular matrix. The SENG is a lymphatic stimulant that increases circulation of the body waste disposal system.

Now, let's take this core program and expand it with the Wheelwright Healing System.

Healing System Factor	Formulas That Address It
1. Constitutional support	Energy Sedate
2. Tissue biochemistry and integrity	ARTA (Jointez)
3. Tissue nourishment	ACCELL, Mpr (Prostata/ Ovata) [nourishes synovial fluid]
4. Pathogen involvements	VRM-2 (Small) #5 (Stabilizer)
5. pH (terrain)	CLR (Chlorophyllium)
6. Drainage	SENG (Lymphogin) + ACCELL
7. Bio-Command Directive	#5 (Stabilizer)

Analysis: Here, a constitutional support formula is chosen along with general terrain and the anti-viral, anti-micotic formula #5 (Stabilizer) brings a powerful, adjunctive contribution. In this comprehensive program, we also add a nutritive formula, the CLR, to help adjust the quality of the blood and the underlying pH.

Example 3: Leaky Gut Syndrome

When pathogenic organisms proliferate in the Gastro-Intestinal tract and foods cause allergenic inflammation of the Gastro-Intestinal tract, the chronic inflammation causes a weakening of the tissue integrity and the intestines become more permeable. When this occurs, the immune system must be on full alert to handle the improperly-digested food molecules that cross into the bloodstream and cause allergenic reactions and fatigue.

Challenge: The program must address the dysbiosis or flora imbalance, reduce inflammation, eliminate micro-organisms, reinstate beneficial flora, correct overly alkaline or overly acidic pH imbalance so enzymes can function properly, and help heal the Gastro-Intestinal tissue.

Solution: Design a comprehensive program to address the multitude of factors involved with the Wheelwright Healing System.

Healing System Factor	Formulas That Address It
1. Constitutional support	Earth Sedate
2. Tissue biochemistry and integrity	ACCELL, D (Digestive)
3. Tissue nourishment	ACCELL + DSIR (Intergen)
4. Pathogen involvements	ABC (Acidophilus/Bifidum/ Bulgaricus Complex)
5. pH (terrain)	APHA (pH Control) + ACCELL + ABC
6. Drainage	ACCELL
7. Bio-Command Directives	Sequence of all six Bio-Commands, in suggested order (#'s 5, 4, 3, 2, 6, 1)

Analysis: Here we see the power the Wheelwright Healing System brings with just a few formulas. The ACCELL serves as tissue support, anti-inflammatory agent, anti-pathogenic, and comprehensive healer of the Gastro Intestinal Tract. Additional support to the healing endeavor comes from DSIR (Intergen) and the #6 (Healer) when it cycles into the program.

Summary. The keys to these three programs are the Bio-Challenge formulas combined with the benefits of the Bio-Command directive.

Next is a guide to the Bio-Challenge formulas by category so you can understand the powerful dimension Wheelwright brought to herbal medicine with formulas that tackle the very difficult, but all-important topics of today's health challenges.

Guide to the Wheelwright Bio-Challenge Formulas

Anti-Pathogenic / Immune Support

ATAK - IMMUNE REJUVENATOR - This formula supports and stimulates the body's immune system. It assists the body to rid itself of entrenched and mutated pathogenic organisms. It provides important support for the lymphatic system. Often, ATAK is included in programs using formulas GOLD, #3, #4, and/or VIVI; in these combinations, the ATAK Formula increases the indicated effectiveness of each.

GOLD - SHIELD PLUS - This formula is a powerful herbal anti-bacterial that operates through a complex process of providing cellular stain markers that inhibits pathogenic bacterial reproduction. This process enhances and improves the body's natural immune system.

VIVI - VIROX - This formula is a natural provider of anti-viral and anti-staph capabilities; it is based on the American Blackfoot and Brazilian native Indian traditions. It contains Leptotoenia and Pau d'Arco and is a specific for acute viral, and bacterial conditions.

VRM1 - LARGE - This formula is for the treatment of larger parasitic organisms in the large intestine.

VRM2 - SMALL - For the treatment of small, blood based foreign life forms and small parasites in the body as well as the G.I. Tract and outer tissues. The formula contains herbal vermifuges affecting nematodes that infest the large intestine as well as blood borne parasitic infestations.

VRM3 - MICRO - This formula assures good health in the intestinal tract by helping the body eliminate single cell pathological and foreign organisms. Often used with three drops of WO oil in a capsule; it combats microscopic parasites including *giardia*.

VRM4 - CELL - This formula is effective in treating cases of cellular and tissue-roaming parasites including amoebas and other protozoan micro-organisms; excellent for handing flukes in the liver and kidney. Often used with three drops of WO oil in a capsule.

Arthritis

ARTA - JOINTEZ - This formula provides anti-pathogenic herbs as well as traditional bio chemical support for assistance in the relief of pain, stiffness, and the daily trauma of arthritis. Often combined with Formula EE for topical pain management.

Blood Building

BLDB (TONIC) - Support for healthy blood; supplies nutrients that encourage general regulation. Particularly effective when used with CLR (Chlorophyllium).

Cells- Cellular Deep Cleansers

OXAA - ORGANIZER CELL - This is a formula that provides deep cellular cleansing detoxification (liver, bones, breast and prostate) that supports any liver program.

OXCC - CLEANSER CELL - This formula carries herbal-based oxygen into the deep tissue to disrupt abnormal activity. It assists by combining of the characteristics of healthy cells as it normalizes, maintains and cleanses.

OXOX - ACTIVATOR C - activates cleansing of deep tissue infections; it provides lymphatic drainage, anti-infective properties, and broad based cleansing of blood and lymph. It is based upon the Moki American Indian herbal cleansing tradition.

Gastro-Intestinal Soothing, Healing

DIJS - ACIDEZE - Provides digestive support that helps break the antacid habit . It helps restore the circadian rhythm of digestion through nutritional support that retrains the body's natural digestive processes. When taken fifteen minutes before eating, DIJS helps control acid indigestion and flatulence.

DSIR - INTERGEN - Supports a healthy rebuilding of tissues and organs. It supports necessary levels of epithelial cells in tissues and organs and supplies nutrients for the Stomach-Duodenal-Thyroid triad, and especially for the G.I. Tract.

Heavy Metal Detoxification

CLNZ - TOXIN CHELATOR - Helps chelate and remove harmful environmental toxins from the tissues, organs, and glands while providing drainage elements. Effective for heavy-metal detoxification (mercury, lead, nickel, aluminum, beryllium, excessive copper, and other toxic chemicals found in the modern environment) through liver and lymph drainage.

Kidney Congestion / Water Balance

KDIR - FLUIDREN - A gentle but highly effective kidney diuretic and stimulant. It supports healthy kidney activity and helps the body sustain appropriate fluid levels. It also aids the kidney process fluids, and helps to remove kidney stones by a natural process of dissolution. KDIR works well with formulas K or Ks for relieving edema and pre-menstrual water-weight gain.

Lymphatic Circulation

SENG - LYMPHOGIN - A lymphatic adjuster that also provides added energy. Southwest American Indian Red Ginseng is balanced with other nutrients to best utilize its ability to cleanse and stimulate the entire lymphatic system; it is also a glandular toner and decongestant.

Muscle Support

KYRO - MUSCLE/LIGAMENT/TISSUE - This formula aids in the strengthening of ligaments, muscles and tissues, and is effective in relieving pain associated with sports injuries and work out regimens. KYRO supports the rebuilding of good, quality muscle after sports and exercise exertion. It also supplies effective support for weakened areas requiring chiropractic adjustment.

pH Balance

APHA (pH CONTROL) - The body's chemistry manager, APHA supports a healthful pH value; it adjusts acid/alkaline levels in the body to a normal state. In cases requiring neutralizing of alkalosis, this formula is often combined with formula Ga (Adrenal); and for excessive, systemic acidity, it is combined with CLR (Chlorophyllium).

The Wheelwright Bio-Nutriment Formulas

Wheelwright researched various nutrients seeking methods of enhancing their assimilation and effectiveness. This research continued over many years and resulted in the inclusion of unique herbal catalysts to accompany vitamins and minerals so concentrated supplementation could be more gentle and effective. The Systemic Bio-Nutriments contains the basic vitamin, mineral, essential fatty acids, gastro-intestinal tract beneficial flora, and other important factors each of which are presented in a superior bio-available matrix necessary for attaining and maintaining good health.

Here is a listing of the formulas that Wheelwright perfected.

ABC - ACIDOPHILUS/BIFIDUM/BULGARICUS COMPLEX - This formula balances beneficial flora in the gastro-intestinal tract. Each capsule contains a minimum of two billion each of the following flora; *Lactobacillus acididophilus, Bifido bacterium bifidum, and Lactobacilus bulgaricus* uniquely suspended in a matrix containing fructooligosaccharydes, beta carotene, grape seed extract , vitamin C and vitamin E to ensure survival of these beneficial cultures into the lower intestinal tract. The formula is assayed by Systemic Formulas to assure product viability.

ACP - VITAMIN ACP - This formula is simultaneously a mild cellular detoxifier and collagen builder. It nutritionally supports tissue integrity and strengthens the body's natural immune system & specifically effective on tissues & muscle detoxification. Indicated for use by children and the elderly; it is particularly valuable in winter to provide nutritional support for protection from colds and flu.

ACX - VITAMIN DTX - This formula is a high-potency, broad spectrum detoxifier; the best drainage formula for use in any cleansing and/or detoxification program. Excellent support for assisting in any pathogen elimination program (candida, parasites, viruses, bacteria) specifically effective for organ detoxification. It's a specific for the left lobe of the liver and the kidneys.

AZV - MULTI-VITAMIN AND MINERAL - The all-purpose multi-vitamin, multi mineral, herbally-chelated formula. The water soluble and oil soluble nutrients are presented in separate capsules thereby assuring maximum assimilation. The herbal chelation renders ingredients for maximum effectiveness.

BFO - BORAGE/FLAX/FISH OILS - This formula is rich in natural highly potent Omega 3 (DHA, EPA) and Omega 6 essential fatty acids that not only support general health, but also are useful in anti-inflammatory programs and general relief for premenstrual syndrome. These nutrients also promote healthy blood vessels, joints, and heart, plus cholesterol modulation functions.

BSV - VITAMIN B STRESS COMPLEX - This unique formula is an allergen-free, yeast-free B complex containing vitalizing herbal chelators providing a matrix for natural assimilation by the body. It supplies an abundance of B vitamins, synergistically balanced. Master Herbalist Wheelwright spent many years developing the herbal-vitamin combination to assure proper catalysts for the vitamin factors.

CAL - CALCIUM PLUS - Ten separate sources of calcium blended with magnesium and Vitamins C, D and E, plus Lecithin satisfies the body's need for the easiest assimilation of calcium. The multi-source calcium provides multiple opportunities for different calcium chelates to be easily absorbed in the G. I. Tract in order to assure adequate amounts of calcium for a healthy body system.

CHLOROPHYLLIUM - This formula is often used as a bacteriostat and soothing agent for relief of inflamed mucus membranes. It provides photosynthetic pigment for mucus membrane balance. High in natural magnesium, it is effective for blood building and balancing properties. It supports a healthy stomach, colon, mucous membranes, allergies and blood coagulation properties. Chlorophyllium also helps to minimize the body's odors.

CTV - VITAMIN C - Five different sources of Vitamin C balanced with Vitamin A, Potassium and anti-bacterial agent, thymol iodide, to provide nutritional support for all conditions in which Vitamin C complex is necessary. Provides sustained activities of Vitamin C with specific application for the immune system's anti-infective processes.

EZV - 200 IU VITAMIN E - A truly, 100% natural Vitamin E provided in a pleasant, chewable form that optimizes assimilation; most often taken between meals or at the beginning of a meal. Its chewable form offers rapid, sub-lingual assimilation maximizes its anti-oxidant results.

FLX - VEGETABLE FLAX SEED OIL - An organic source of Omega-3 and Omega-6 fatty acids that help properly transport calcium and providing specific heart support. It helps sustain healthy levels of cholesterol, provides relief of arthritic pain, and is essential in building and strengthening general glandular and hormonal functions.

LEV - LECITHIN - A source of phospholipids needed by the brain, heart, nerves, liver, and joints. Helps facilitate restful sleep, assists mental functions and promotes the growth of healthy hair.

MIN - MULTI MINERAL PLUS - This is a broad-spectrum mineral formula that helps the body maintain its electrolytic balance. It is a source of inland-sea-based trace minerals enhanced in a plant matrix to assure maximum assimilation. A mineral-rich body is a healthy body.

PRO - NUTRO PROTEIN - This formula provides essential amino-acids and peptide chains commonly deficient in today's average diet; it enhances and completes dietary protein structures thus allowing the body to assimilate up to three times more protein without added fats and carbohydrates through a process of enhancing and easing protein absorption. PRO preserves the lymphatic nucleoprotein pool essential to healthy body functions.

PTM - POTASSIUM STABILIZER - This formula is a natural, plant-source of potassium. It provides balanced, healthful blood levels of potassium and magnesium while providing support for muscles (especially the heart), nerves, brain, hair and skin. It helps regulate water and electrolyte balance as well as sodium levels. Provides support for weight loss programs.

REL - SUPER CHLORELLA - This formula supports all body systems and aids stabilization during a general body-cleansing program and helps maintain a healthy immune system. It provides factors important for cellular detoxification and is especially useful in heavy metal detoxification programs. It's also a good source for protein and a good blood builder.

ZNC - ZINC CHELATE - This formula is a valuable, natural source of elemental zinc which is the key to effective digestive enzymes, reproductive organ development, and proper hormone production. ZNC helps the male reproductive organs. Serves as a tally to determine if adequate zinc is available in the body.

Bio-Extract Formulas

The Wheelwright Bio-Extract Formulas include oils and liquids that help with many common day-to-day challenges including skin problems, internal disorders, bruises, scratches, cuts, and immune challenges.

AO - ALOE VERA - This product is a quadruple concentration extracted from the inner gel (inside the leaves, thus omitting the toxic properties of the outer leaf) of the Aloe Vera plant. It provides potent, natural healing factors. It is used both as a cosmetic agent and a healing.

EE - ESSENE ESSENCE OIL - A combination of essential oils used topically for muscles and joints, it's often used to help "hold" chiropractic adjustments. A soothing agent for heart pain and brings relief to aches, pains, headaches, congestion and bruises. This formula is high in "YIN" energy - the receptive, alkalizing bio-energetic force.

EV - ELIXER VITA - An energy-boosting formula that eases allergies, colds and builds flu resistance, EV serves to nutritionally boost the immune system. It fights bacterial infections and helps cleanse the system. Diluted with juice, it is excellent for children and elderly people. It contains powerful immune system strengthening herbs.

IA - IMPERIAL ATAKER - This tincture fights sub-clinical diseases and enhances the body's natural shield system. It is equally effective for children. Deriving its properties from the successful ATAK formula, its liquid transport provides rapid uptake of essential healing factors.

RV - RENAVATOR - This non-emulsified oil combination provides a natural healing matrix for toning the skin. It is an effective healing emollient, skin soother and moisturizer that is used for treating rashes, sunburn, and burns. It effectively moisturizes repairs and brings relief to dry chapped and/or sunburned skin and is effectively used for hemorrhoid and vaginal dryness.

TR - TAI RA CHI - This liquid formula is an ultra-high energy cellular energizer, anti-viral, anti-fungal and anti-bacterial. This is a premium anti-fungal extract derived from polarity-corrected Brazilian Pau d'Arco. Using a catalytic process of distillation and extraction, Formula

TR uses the powerful energies contained in the bark of the genuine Pau d'Arco tree of the Brazilian rain forest.

WO - CHINA HEALING OIL - A first aid kit in a bottle, its many properties make it essential for the modern-day medicine chest High in "Yang" energy - the active, stimulating bio-energetic force, WO is effective for treatment of sore throat, wounds, abrasions, cuts, bruises, as an anti-diarrheal, and for relief of general gastro-intestinal malaise. WO is also effective against parasites.

SC - CLEANSER - This formula cleanses persistent infections; it is the skin-blemish fighting formula. Use topically as a wet dressing for acne, skin rashes, chicken pox, poison ivy, poison oak, etc.. Also used diluted in water as a douche for vaginal yeast infections.

Concentrated Extracts

Systemic Formulas' concentrated extracts are highly-effective, liquid-based derivatives of the successful capsulated formulations. They are carefully produced by Stu Wheelwright, Jr. to assure that all essential factors in the original formula are present. The CX formulas offer several benefits:

1. Suitable for those who have difficulty taking capsules or tablets.
2. Assimilate rapidly (including sublingually).
3. May be given in micro and/or macro dosages.
4. May be added to spring water, juices, or other beverages.

CX1 - Activator: Dramatically increases effectiveness of other formulas.

CX2 - Builder: Promotes cellular health and healing.

CX3 - Bactrex: Assists in handling infections assuring cellular health.

CX4 - FungDX: A cellular neutralizer of toxins and waste materials.

CX5 - Stabilize: Normalizes and stabilizes healthy cell growth,

CX6 - Restore: Supports the body's innate effective healing.

CXB - Brain: Healthy brain support for increased mental effectiveness.

CXF+ - Female Plus: Supports healthy menstrual rhythm relieving problems.

CXFpms - Female Health: Supports a healthy female hormonal balance.

CXGa - Adrenal: Provides a healthy balance of the body's chemistry.

CXGb - Pituitary/Pineal: Supports a healthful pituitary function.

CXGf - Thyroid: Provides long-term health through thyroid support.

CXGt - Thymus: Strengthens the thymus.

CXH - Heart: Supports heart health and strength.

CXHn - Heart Nerve: Assists maintenance of the bundle branch system.

CXI - Eyes: Supports a clear and healthy vision system.

CXK - Kidney: Supports healthy kidneys.

CXL - Liver: Total support for the healthy Liver and Gall Balder.

CXLb - Liver/Gall Bladder: Blood purification for liver processes.

CXLs - Liver S: Promotes health in the liver through toxin chelation.

CXM+ - Male Endocrine: Male glandular rebuilding formula.

CXMpc - Prostata Corrector: Provides nutrients for prostate health.

CXN3 - Relaxa: A nervine that provides pain relief.

CXNc - Calm: Promotes healthy and clam nerves.

CXP - Pancreas: Provides nutritional support for healthy pancreatic functions.

CXR - Lung: Nutritional support for relief of respiratory dysfunction.

CXS - Spleen: Provides support for the Spleen-Pancreas-liver triad.

CXACX - Vitamin Detox: Provides effective support for any cleansing program.

CXAPHA - pH Control: Normalizes the acid/alkaline balance in the body.

CXCLNZ - Chelator: Chelates heavy metal toxins form the body.

CXGOLD - Immune Plus: A balanced broad and intense anti-bacterial.

CXOXAA - Cell Organizer: Detoxifier. Deep tissue cellular support.

CXOXCC - Cleanser Cell: Provides healthy cellular cleansing and maintenance.

CXOXOX - Activator cell: Encourages release of toxins on a deep cellular level.

CXSENG - Lymphogin: Stimulates natural drainage of the lymph.

CXVIVI - Anti-Viro: Powerful anti-viral and anti-bacterial formula.

CXVRM1 - Large: Provides health through handling large parasites.

CXVRM2 - Small: Provides health through handling small parasites.

CXVRM3 - Micro: Provides health through handling micro-pathogens.

CXVRM4 - Cell: Provides health through handling cellular pathogens.

Biopathic Formulas

Bio-Pathic formulas are based on subtle, molecular bio-nutrition via bio-energetic ingredients.

COLD - ZINCASTOP - Taken at the first sign of impending discomfort, this formula aids in the prevention/ relief of cold symptoms, sore throats, and allaying further infection form developing.

ZC - ZIN CHI - This formula is essential in establishing energy signatures within the body structure for diagnostic purposes in utilizing such tools as the Computron® and/or the Listen® bio-diagnostic equipment.

Chinese Dragon Rising 5-Element Formulas

Doc Wheelwright applied his mastery of Chinese herbology to create a group of formulas that effectively marry Eastern wellness philosophy with bio-energetic principles for comprehensive, constitutional support. These Dragon Rising Formulas enable the health practitioner to combine the best in Eastern herbal healing and health philosophies with a refined bio-energetic enhancement.

GENERAL SEDATE - Relieve Depression - Relieves stagnation of nervous system, balances the general energy & emotional state of the body. Sedates and nourishes yin of the lungs, kidneys, spleen and liver for general health. Cleanse excess heat; disperse the liver; cleanse heart fire.

GENERAL TONIFY - Generate The Pulse - Tonifies and nourishes lungs, spleen, kidneys and liver. Tonifies and invigorates the blood for general glandular health. Helps to make positive changes of habit and increases general circulation & vitality. Tonify Qi; nourishes the blood; raise pulse; tonify kidney yang; strengthen the lungs and spleen.

ENERGY SEDATE - Clear Heat - Anti-stress formula for health of the throat, skin, lymph, and eyes. Supports lymphatics. Clean heat and drain fire; nourish yin.

ENERGY TONIFY - Tonify Yin - Tonifies throat, skin, lymph, and eyes to support and balance health. Balances male and female energy.

EARTH SEDATE - Clear Congestion - Sedation points for the spleen and stomach. Has anti-viral properties, helps with stress. Anti-stress formula. Enrich yin; nourish the stomach; drain excel stomach fire; dispense food and assuage stagnation.

EARTH TONIFY - Warm The Center - Source and tonfication points for the stomach and spleen. Reduces sugar cravings. Strengthens the health of the spleen, kidneys, and digestive system. Boost the Qi; fortify the spleen; warm the yang and reinforce movement; uplift the yang.

FIRE SEDATE - Pacify The Spirit - Sedation Points for heart, small intestine; the triple warmer, and heart constrictor. Relieves stress of the heart, kidneys, and nervous system. Drains heart fire; breakdown of cardio-renal interaction; enrich Yin and lessen fire.

FIRE TONIFY - Support The Heart - Heart 7 (Spirit Gate), conception vessel. Helps body create an anti-parasitic environment. Supports and strengthens the health of the heart and blood circulation. Support the heat Qi; nourish the heart and quiet the spirit; warm and free heart yang.

METAL SEDATE - Ventilate The Lungs - Sedation Points for the Lungs and Large Intestine. Anti-bacterial, hyper-immune, activity of lungs. Peaceful breathing; clears and calms the throat, coughing, lungs and respiratory functions for overall health. Diffuse the lung; purify and relieve the lungs.

METAL TONIFY - Support The Weak And Thin - Source and tonification for the large intestine and lungs. Supports the weak and thin; strengthens the lungs, spleen, and throat for general health. Supplement yang Qi; diffuse the lungs; enrich yin and moisten the lungs.

WATER SEDATE - Remove Dampness - Sedation points for the kidneys and bladder. Removes dampness; relieves stress in kidneys, spleen, and digestive system to provide a healthy balance. Warms the kidneys; restore yang; transforms damp.

WATER TONIFY - Strengthen Bones - Source and tonification points for the kidney and bladder. Strengthens bones; supports health of kidneys, spleen, digestive system and connective tissues. Supplement the kidneys; boosts the essence; enrich the kidneys and nourish yin.

WOOD SEDATE - Mediate Harmony - Sedation points for the liver and gall bladder. Anti-fungal. Calms tension in the liver, blood, spleen and digestion allowing healthy functions. Cool the blood; sedate liver yang rising; calm the liver and extinguish wind; harmonize the liver and spleen; course the liver and harmonize the stomach.

WOOD TONIFY - Tonify Blood - Source for the liver and gall bladder. Strengthens the blood, improves resistance to allergies; supports the healthy liver and blood. Nourish liver-blood; enrich kidney's yin; subdue yang.

Appendix D

What makes Wheelwright's Systemic Forumlas® Unique

1. **Herbal Polarity.** Wheelwright spent over 35 years researching the compatibility of herbs. He found that herbs have a polarity in their direction of influence on the body—stimulators, sedators, and tonics. Wheelwright established laws that govern how to combine the herbs for the greatest effectiveness with the least amount of side effects. When to combine a anionic herbal mixture with a cationic element to buffer its influence or vice-versa was based on bio-energetic analysis of the combined properties, and then tested with thousands of people.

2. **Bio-Energetic Compatibility.** Each organ, gland, and body system resonates at a uniquely identifiable energy level. Wheelwright selected and combined herbs and other nutritive factors to be compatible with the targeted tissue. More than that, he designed his formulas to resonate to the optimal bioenergetic frequency of the tissue's archetypal blueprint. He found this accomplished an effectiveness that was greater than the sum total of the individual parts.

3. **Quality for Life.** Wheelwright found that only the highest quality, natural ingredients support and sustain the life force of the resulting formulas. "Quality is everything in nutrition." This recognition of the life factors in nutrition is continued by his son, Stuart, Jr., with a dedication to the proper harvesting, transport, warehousing, and manufacture of his father's formulations.

4. **Multi-Faceted Nutrition.** More than herbs, Wheelwright formulations contain other natural, nutritive factors that enhance the healing potentials of the herbs or the herbs enhance their healing potentials. Ingredients such as vitamins, minerals, amino acids, cellular identity factors, fatty acids, saccharides, enzymes, and other nutritive factors are often combined into the herbal matrix for greater assimilation and utilization by the body.

5. **Smaller dosages.** The precision in the balance and energy of Wheelwright's formulas, and the compatibility with the body's innate energies, results in formulas that do more with less. With the right energy, the body's own healing resources contribute to the formula-initiated process.

6. **The healing power of herbs.** As life-determined structures, plants learn to adapt and survive in a competitive environment. This innate resilience is what makes herbs a primary healing influence for the human being. Their innate ability to cleanse (stimulate), build (sedate), and sustain health has been demonstrated for thousands of years. Systemic formulas are based on the therapeutic matrices of herbs, enhanced by the bioenergetic and biochemical research of A.S. Wheelwright.

7. **Bio-Energetic Beacon.** The energy matrix of a Wheelwright formula provides an instantaneous 'wake up call' to the body to correct and improve the tissue integrity of the targeted organ or gland. It serves as a beacon to the body to effect the necessary corrections to restore the most optimal health possible.

8. **Targeted nutrition.** The Bio-Function formulas provide a neutral, balanced, therapy for the regeneration and healing of the targeted tissue. Through bio-energy and cellular identity factors, Wheelwright found that properly-designed formulas could deliver more nutritional healing components to the tissue for its maintenance and repair.

9. **Specific directive to the targeted tissue.** The six Bio-Command formulas provide a specific enhancement to other formulas (specifically the Bio-Function formulas) thus allowing the practitioner the prerogative of a specific focus for even faster results.

10. **Tried and True.** Wheelwright's formulas have been used for over 30 years. Thousands of doctors have used his formulas with hundreds of thousands of people. To date, six companies have copied Wheelwright's early formulations in an attempt to equal his proven effectiveness. However, his finest work, the Systemic Formulas, are exclusively made available to health practitioners only by Systemic Formulas, Inc.

11. **Brazilian herbs.** Wheelwright was a master of many herbal systems from around the world including Chinese, Native American, Aruvedic, but it was in the Brazilian, Amazon-region herbs that he found the most consistently vital, pristine, and nascent healers. Thus, his Systemic formulas often include a matrix of South American herbs.

12. **The Wheelwright Healing System.** Wheelwright made his formulas compatible with each other. In his system of natural healing, the multi-faceted support necessary to heal and restore health is found in the interlinking of his formula categories supporting the body including the general (constitutional) state, the specific tissue integrity, and the therapeutic application to address a known cause.

Appendix E

A Life of Service to Humanity
A Brief Biography of A.S. Wheelwright

Born, 1918 in Utah, the son of a contractor.

Recognized precocious. Spoke first words as complete sentences. Learned to read before attending school and showed an immediate and unquenchable interest in science.

Showed early affinity for herbs and plants. In early grade school, lead the class on herb walks in the foothills of the Wasach Mountains. He exhibited an innate knowing of plants and their medicinal properties.

Age 10. Received a large chemistry set. Checked out texts on Applied Chemistry from the local library and 'consumed' books on chemistry for the next few years. He went on to build one of the finest chemistry laboratories in the Western United States by age 19.

Age 13. To finance his expanding chemistry lab, Wheelwright raised 40,000 black widow spiders and set up a venom extraction system. He sent the venom to the Florida Tropical Disease Research Center where scientists there were able to develop anti-venom and supply it to the world.

Developed and published information on sprouting seeds (clover, radish, alfalfa, etc.) for a highly nutritious survival food.

Age 17. Received the prestigious Edison Award for being the most outstanding Applied Chemistry student in the United States.

Age 18 - 22. Attended college in Utah (Weber College 1936-1939), Utah State University (Logan, UT 1939-1941), Armed Forces Institute 1941, and later attended University of Hawaii and Christian University Arizona. (Ph.D.Chemistry).

Age 21. Produced a milestone paper covering 10 vitamins, their use, effect and utilization by the body. This report was used as the authoritative reference guide for several years.

Age 25. Served as an explosives chemist in the armed forces (USAF) during WWII in the South Pacific theater.

Returned from the war with a rare form of 'jungle rot'. Hospitalized, expected to die. After months on antibiotics, began "prayer and fasting" regimen along with diet and herbs and recovered his health. Dedicated his live to discovering how to heal and how to live a healthy life. "I knew that I had been given the answer to my incurable illness and had been given the charge to use natural herbs not only to help myself, but also, and more importantly, to help mankind return to a state of well-ness."

Age 26-28. Armed Services School of Technology (USN)

Employed by Eastman Kodak as a member of their Research Panel. Also by the U.S. Department of Engineers and by Betty Crocker. He developed over 400 patented concepts for food and fodder.

U.S. Government appointed him to a counsel on radiation survival techniques (post atomic attacks.)

Taught survival skills as a school curriculum.

Extensive research on the effects of diet on body chemistry.

Age 38. Hospitalized, cholera.

Worked with Adele Davis (California), and later with Dr. Royal Lee. While with Dr. Lee, he taught nutrition classes for Chiropractors. Suggested to Dr. Lee that herbs be incorporated into the nutritional, therapeutic programs that Lee was researching and designing.

Wheelwright returned to Utah and built Life Factors, a multi-million dollar company to formulate nutritional supplements using the healing properties of herbs. (Now defunct.)

General research and accomplishments include:

- Developed the Lo-stress diet, the precursor to the Pro-Vita diet.
- Discovered the body chemistry cyclic response patterns.
- Advanced world knowledge on pH (acid/alkaline balance) pertaining to oxygen utilization, calcium metabolism, and arthritis; as well as documented the pH reversal swing in cancer.

- Developed the basic theorem of the relationship between dominant and recessive DNA in the developing zygote.
- Developed the Rational Diet in 1959, applying nutritional theories 30-years ahead of their time.
- The first to promote American Red Ginseng and Chaparral as lymphatic cleansing agents; and myrtle as effective for leukemia.
- One of the first health authorities to recognize and treat the fungal/parasitic symbiotic relationship in chronic degenerative disease.
- Applied Kirlian techniques to develop natural pain alleviation treatments.
- Advanced the charting of the electro-lymphatic system and its relationship to acupuncture, reflexology.
- Developed the correlation between temperature (as an index of tissue disorder) and functionality.
- Developed "The Food Factory" - a hydroponics system for family use utilizing organic methods.
- Invented practical methods for growing high protein foods in desert lands.
- Discovered ten 'new' plants that could be introduced into the human food chain as foods.
- Developed the art and science of Sclerology - the interpretation of the red lines in the whites of the eyes for their health implications.
- Developed Dermataglyphics - the art and science of interpreting the reflex lines on the soles of the feet for their health implications.
- Patented inventions in the photographic industry.
- Developed theories on Bio-Magnetism and instruments to use crystal/magnetic energy for healing.
- Perfected Systemic Formulas.
- 1990. Died peacefully at his Utah home after an herbal expedition in Baja California, Mexico.

P.S. In his studies with the Native Americans (Wheelwright was a Medicine Man in two tribes), it was the Nez Perce chief who, after teaching Wheelwright the Mirror Technique method of impressing the subconscious mind to overcome limitations (information presented in the book, *Passion Play*) gave Wheelwright his commission regarding his work as a healer:

> *The movement of the White Eyes' medicine turns*
> *from the broad to the narrow,*
> *the general to the specific,*
> *the large to the minute,*
> *concentric rings,*
> *each inside the other,*
> *until it has become confined, stagnant, standing still.*
>
> *May you walk in ever-broader circles,*
> *each surrounding the former,*
> *until your message encompasses the universe.*

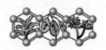

For a complete training course
in Wheelwright's Systemic Herbology,
see www.apple-a-daypress.com

Apple-A-Day Press

"Dedicated to the Healing of the Whole Person"

Books ● Courses ● Natural Health Programs ● Videos ● CDs ● Lab Tests

www.apple-a-daypress.com

Wilby © 2001

Apple-A-Day Press

1500 Village West Drive, Suite 77
Austin, TX 78733
Phone: 512-328-3996
Toll Free: 877-442-7753
Fax: 512-263-7787
E-mail: apple-a-day@austin.rr.com

Welcome to Apple-A-Day Press:
Your natural health resource!

Here you'll find some of the most amazing and informative books, courses, and healing programs available in the world today!

Since 1984, Apple-A-Day Press has published insightful books and natural health courses that have helped thousands (even millions) of people with their health. With a primary focus on the research and writings of Dr. Jack Tips, nothing here is like what you've encountered before. At Apple-A-Day, you'll view health and healing from a totally new perspective—one that is deeper, more well-rounded, and watch out—you may catch a dose of dry Texas humor! These books are jam-packed with valuable information that truly brings the gift of health.

You'll find much more information on our web site, www.apple-a-daypress.com including downloads of chapters of our books, other free articles, lab tests, nutritional programs, and health building tools.

It is indeed an honor and a pleasure to share these tools, insights and knowledge with you. It is our foremost desire that this site contribute to your good health, good insight, and good life...Best Wishes in your health endeavors!

Apple-A-Day Press

Natural Healing at Your Fingertips

For more information on your "do it yourself" health improvement system, log on to www.apple-a-daypress.com.

Join the Apple-A-Day Press confidential mailing list and be the first to know about new books, discounts, special offers and seminars. Join on line at www.apple-a-daypress.com.

Toll free order line: 1-877-442-7753
(orders only. 24-hours secure)
Or on-line: www.apple-a-daypress.com

APPLE-A-DAY PRESS

1500 Village West Drive, Suite 77, Austin, Texas, 78733
Phone: 512.328.3996 Fax: 512.263.7787
Website: www.apple-a-daypress.com
Email: apple-a-day@austin.rr.com

Passion Play by Dr. Jack Tips

If ever a book could change your life—increase your wealth, improve your relationships, and open your heart—this is it. Absolutely profound and insightful. Believe this—the Mirror Technique is a true shortcut to success in any endeavor. It starts where other self-help books leave off—beyond affirmations, beyond visualization, beyond anything you've ever tried!

Passion Play is the art of combining Sensualization with the Native American Mirror Technique to harness your hidden power of manifestation. Use this technique to awaken your heart, encourage your actions, enliven your dreams, clarify your mission, achieve your goals and discover your true destiny. Passion Play is a new, powerful breakthrough in self-realization and human potential. Wealth, love, romance, success, charity, health, freedom, contentment, joy, excitement and spiritual adventures await you—within these pages, within your life. Never before has the step-by-step process to recreate yourself, create your future life, and follow your heart's desire based on your core values become so clear, simple, and effective. Now you can discover your passion and begin your play. Passion Play will improve your life—Forever.

333 pages, ISBN 0-929167-20-1 $24.95

The Weight Is Over by Dr. Jack Tips

A powerful, health-building book. The last weight-loss book you'll ever need! Much more than how to lose weight, this book teaches how to gain true health! Anyone can benefit from this myth-busting breakthrough!

Get trim now! It's not your fault your weight is up and your energy is down. You've avoided fat, you've increased grains, you've eaten less—just like they told you. But you know what? They told you wrong! Now, for the first time, find out why people have excessive weight and how you can eradicate it. Learn about the perfect, custom-designed eating plan for you as an individual! Take The FitTest—a simple, in-home lab test that reveals how to get trim now. The Weight Is Over is a groundbreaking new program that takes you step by step into a mastery of nutrition—both eating to lose fat and building optimal health simultaneously. Much more than a crash program, this book helps you build a healthy Pro-Vita! lifestyle that will benefit you for the rest of your life. Learn about:

- So called "bad" foods that are really good for you!
- Super foods that unleash your body's ability to burn fat while you sleep!
- Herbs and nutrients that help you burn fat for energy!
- 'Syndrome X' and how it silently kills people.
- The 12 Optimal Food Factors – never before published insights on everything your diet must provide you to prevent disease and be healthy!

The Weight Is Over is more than guidelines and tips, it is a strategic action plan, based on over 30-years of research and clinical experience. You'll be taken through the maze of nutrition confusion into a very simple, crystal clear program that brings you success you can keep. It's easy, it's fun, it's effective!

300 pages (limited edition), ISBN 0-929167-21-X $24.95

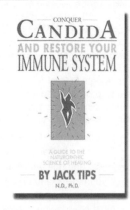

Breast Health – A Women's Health Discourse by Dr. Jack Tips

Are you simply waiting and hoping your next mammogram won't steal your life with the dreaded news? Find out what you can do now to not only protect your health but to have overall female hormone balance. Find out why men need to read this material.

From the natural health perspective, there are clear reasons that breast cancer occurs and thus there are clear steps to take to prevent it! In this discourse, you will learn the reasons that the breast tissue is susceptible to disease and learn simple steps to avoid them. Beyond disease concerns, the breasts play an important role in overall female hormonal balance. Breast health is an important part of overcoming PMS, menstrual cramping, endometriosis, and menopausal symptoms. This discourse discusses the role of breast tissue in female endocrine balance and demonstrates how to maintain healthy breast tissue. Features the breast-test and breast massage technique to help prevent breast disease and maintain tissue integrity. Unpublished manuscript.

56 pages, illustrations $9.95

The Next Step to Greater Energy: A Unique Perspective on Bioenergy, Addictions and Transformation by Dr. Jack Tips

Are your "little addictions" a clear symptom of a metabolic imbalance? Breaking addictive behaviors is more effective with this information.

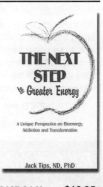

Explore the energy systems of the body with emphasis on both the glandular (thyroid and adrenals) and bio-electric energy systems. This book presents a new look at the connection between bio-energy and addictions. Discover energy impostors including substances, activities, and habits. Identify addictions and habits as symptoms of bio-energetic and biochemical imbalances. Discover the true cause of cravings and addictive patterns, and how to correct the underlying imbalances. How to stop smoking is thoroughly discussed. The focus of this practical information is how to obtain freedom and fuller spiritual expression.

Web download only, www.apple-a-daypress.com, 210 pages, index, ISBN 0-929167-04-X $16.95

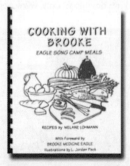
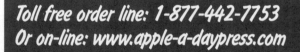

A Guidebook to Clinical Nutrition for the Health Professional by Dr. Timothy Kuss

What to do and how to do it. Valuable information on how to help people heal.

A fascinating guide and desk reference through Dr. Wheelwright's work with herbs by one of his leading protégés. Includes a 400-entry Clinician's Manual of herbal protocols, and demonstrates Dr. Wheelwright's bioenergetic research. Full of valuable information on the natural cure of the most common health concerns. Includes more than the Wheelwright herbal system and embraces the full spectrum of natural healing.

Revised in 2001, 275 pages $21.95

Systemic Nutrition/Herbology Training Program (The Training!) by Dr. Jack Tips with Dr. Tim Kuss

Master the Doc Wheelwright healing formulas and learn his programming secrets with this cassette course that becomes your desk reference book for one of the most advanced healing systems in the world.

For the health professional, this training program features 14 cassette tapes, a discourse on advanced applications of Doc Wheelwright's herbal system, and a 200-page desk reference for thorough training in the applications of Wheelwright's research and Systemic Herbal Formulas. Reveals Wheelwright's secrets about how and why he created his famous herbal healing combinations. You will quickly become proficient in comprehensive program design using Wheelwright's complete healing system. This program will make you a master of systemic herbology. (The Training is a prerequisite for the Health Professionals' 2nd Opinion Program.)

14 cassettes in binder, discourse (protocols), 200-page manual $159.00

For additional health professional offerings, please visit www.jacktips.com

Blood Chemistry & Clinical Nutrition by Dr. Jack Tips

Deep nutritional insights from the ordinary Auto-Chem, SMAC-26/CBC blood test.

For the clinical nutritionist, this manual and desk reference examines each blood test value from the SMAC-26/CBC lab test for its nutritional health implications and provides Systemic Formulas protocols for correcting imbalances. Includes optimal values, pathologies, clinical notes, cross-references, protocols and valuable insights from other clinicians. An absolutely essential tool for the practicing health professional.

123 pages, ISBN 0-929167-07-4 $44.95

Insights in the Eyes: An Introduction to Sclerology by Dr. Jack Tips

Once you know these signs in the whites of the eye, you have insights about the cause of a person's constitution and the chief factors that can limit health.

A brief but thorough introduction to the history, premises, and practice of interpreting the red lines in the white of the eyes for stress patterns and nutritional implications. Features the 30 most common stress lines, commentaries, and excerpts from the ISI Art & Science of Sclerology Certification Course.

90 pages, illustrations $19.95

The Art & Science of Sclerology Certification Course by Dr. Jack Tips

Red lines in the whites of your eyes—what do they mean? Here's the most accurate, most advanced, most comprehensive, and most simple training in Sclerology—the interpretation of the red lines in the whites of the eyes for their health implications!

You can become a Sclerologist! Here is the most advanced up-to-date information in the world on the interpretation of the red lines in the white of the eyes for their health implications. This course will certify you to interpret what the sclera—the whites of the eyes—is revealing about a person's health.

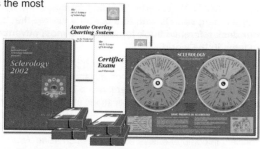

This is the International Sclerology Institute's (ISI's) distance education certification course and is the definitive and foundational course for all Sclerologists around the world. Straight from the founder—A.S. Doc Wheelwright—this course teaches you to master the language of the eyes. It contains 7-hours of instructional video (CD-DVD) along with a segment on the adrenal glands taught by Wheelwright; a 300-page manual, a full-color wall chart, the wall chart depicting organ zones, the acetate overlay system, 6 CD-DVDs of classroom presentation, *Insights In the Eyes* book, calligraphic pen, and certification exam. Upon completion, your certificate is issued and you become a certified Sclerologist. More information is at www.sclerology-institute.org.

Regular price $699
Limited time special offer price $469

Sclerology Pens

Doc Wheelwright's favorite pen for accurately charting the sclera.

This calligraphic pen delivers red ink via a brush on one end plus a fine-line detail via a nib on the other end. Perfect to capture the prominent veins as well as fine lines and other markings when charting the sclera on paper.

$3.95 each

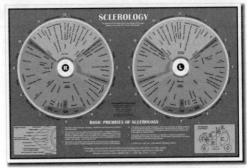
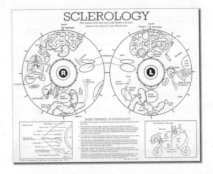

Sclerascope (Sclerology/Iridology) Camera

The ancient science enters the 21st Century! State of the art camera puts sclera (and iris) images on your computer screen for grid analysis and more.

Take advantage of instant photography for immediate analysis with direct input into your own personal computer or laptop. This state of the art instrument has been built to the precise specifications of leading iridologists worldwide and its applications are perfectly applicable for Sclerology.

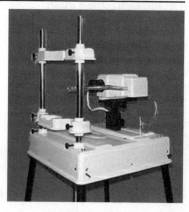

Unlock and capture the history and all the vital information portrayed in the sclera through the use of the Sclerascope Camera System. It's fast, safe and easy to operate. This complete, turnkey system utilizes the patented, fiber optic, proper spectrum lighting system (180,000 optical fibers) designed for close-up macro enlargements of the sclera (and iris). This unique high intensity, cool lighting system captures the greatest depth of field and the highest resolution, offering the most comfort and protection to the eyes against the dangers of ultra-violet rays that are produced from all photography lighting.

Now you can photograph your patient's sclera (and iris) with this digital camera system and bring it to your computer screen for immediate analysis during the time of visit. This camera system comes with the renowned Iridology Scanning System software included (a $495 value) and a USB connector plug-in—everything you need to operate the camera, to view, enhance and examine the eye's information on the screen.

High Resolution, up to 1.2 million pixels. The image comes directly into your computer. Compatible with Windows 98 for the PC and the Virtual PC program on the Apple/Macintosh.

This 120 volts system is lightweight, yet durable, can be operated on location under any lighting conditions or is completely mobile for easy set-up and use wherever you might travel. (Optional 220V adapters available.)

Features:

- Telescoping legs and supporting platform
- Chin and head rests for customer comfort
- State of the art digital/video camera. (No previous photography experience necessary)
- Two fiber optical lighting assemblies with macro enlargement lenses
- Travel case
- Complete instruction manual
- One year limited warranty
- Operating System—Iridology Scanning Software. You receive a complete iris scanning grid system to which you will add the independent Sclerology plug in. Features:

Sclerascope Camera Photos

Travel Case

  - Patient Database: records patient details, sclera (and iris) signs, suggestions and comments
  - Patient Report Printouts: Includes the option to print out patient sclera and iris images, graphs, suggestions, comments and sclera markings
  - Image Adjustment: through a selection of settings
  - State of the art tools including: Graphic and Text Tools, Image Zooming Tools, Diets, Help files on Constitutions
  - Sclerology Interpretive CD-ROM Software (List: $349. Included.)

Regular price $5950   ISI price $5650.

Apple-A-Day Press
Dedicated to the Healing of the Whole Person

Important News! Our web site www.apple-a-daypress.com offers additional health-enhancing services including Lab Tests, Tried 'N True Nutritional Programs, and Natural Resources (health building products) to bring you more tools for optimal health.

ORDER FORM

Books and Tapes

- The Weight Is Over* (ISBN 0-929167-21-x) .... $24.95 _____ $ _____
- Passion Play* (ISBN 0-929167-20-1) .... $24.95 _____ $ _____
- The Pro-Vita! Plan for Optimal Nutrition* (ISBN 0-929167-05-8) .... $22.95 _____ $ _____
- Conquer Candida – Restore Your Immune System* (ISBN 0-929167-00-7) .... $15.95 _____ $ _____
- Breast Health – Women's Health Discourse .... $9.95 _____ $ _____
- The Next Step to Greater Energy* (ISBN 9-929167-04-X) (web download)...... $16.95 _____ $ _____
- Your Liver...Your Lifeline! (The Healing Triad)* (ISBN 0-929167-06-6).............. $15.95 _____ $ _____
- The Healing Triad (2 CD set) .... $19.95 _____ $ _____
- The Healing Triad Set (Your Liver...Your Lifeline! book and CDs) .... $32.95 _____ $ _____
- Cooking with Brooke .... $12.00 _____ $ _____

For the Health Professional

- A Guidebook to Clinical Nutrition.. $21.95 _____ $ _____
- Systemic Nutrition/Herbology Training Program (cassettes & manual) .... $159.00 _____ $ _____
- Blood Chemistry & Clinical Nutrition (ISBN 0-929167-07-4)............................ $44.95 _____ $ _____

Sclerology

- Insights in the Eyes: An Introduction to Sclerology* (ISBN 9-929167-11-2) ...... $19.95 _____ $ _____
- The Art & Science of Sclerology Certification Course (list $699) .... $469.00 _____ $ _____
- Sclerology Pens .... $3.95 _____ $ _____
- Sclerology Wall Chart* (Color) .... $19.95 _____ $ _____
- Sclerology Wall Chart* (Organs Depicted) .... $14.95 _____ $ _____
- Sclerology Starter Package (book, CD, chart) .... $49.95 _____ $ _____
- The Art & Science of Sclerology Manual CD-ROM.. $99.95 _____ $ _____

ORDER SUBTOTAL $ _____

> * Discount available with purchase of any combination of 12 or more of titles denoted with an asterix. Contact our office for more information.

TAX (if applicable) $ _____

S&H, COD $ _____

TOTAL $ _____

Name _____Date _____

Address _____

City/State/Zip _____

Phone_____E-mail _____

Method of Payment ☐ Check ☐ Credit Card

Name on card _____

Card # _____

Exp. Date _____

Signature _____

Order on the Internet at: www.apple-a-daypress.com

Apple-A-Day Press
1500 Village West Drive, Suite 77
Austin, TX 78733

E-mail:
apple-a-day@austin.rr.com

Phone: 512-328-3996
Toll Free: 877-442-7753
Fax: 512-263-7787

For a catalog of Systemic Formula's offerings, and more training information, please contact your Systemic Representative

Or call Systemic Formulas
1-800-445-4647
(Health Professionals Only)